An Introduction t

by Paul Foster Case

and Wade Coleman

Edited by Wade Coleman

Copyright 2018 by Wade Coleman

May 2023 Edition

Upon my death, this book enters the Public Domain

ACKNOWLEDGMENTS

Special thanks to Carol Z for her editing.

To contact the author, write to this email.

DENDARA_ZODIAC@protonmail.com

TABLE OF CONTENTS

FOREWORD	5
INTRODUCTION	8
CHAPTER 1 – THE FOOL	12
CHAPTER 2 – THE MAGICIAN	22
CHAPTER 3 – HIGH PRIESTESS	31
CHAPTER 4 – THE EMPRESS	46
CHAPTER 5 – THE EMPERIOR	61
CHAPTER 6 – THE HIEROPHANT	72
CHAPTER 7 – THE LOVERS	83
CHAPTER 8 – THE CHARIOT	95
CHAPTER 9 – STRENGTH	107
CHAPTER 10 – THE HERMIT	117
CHAPTER 11 – WHEEL OF FORTUNE	128
CHAPTER 12 – JUSTICE	143
CHAPTER 13 – HANGED MAN	153
CHAPTER 14 – DEATH	166
CHAPTER 15 – TEMPERANCE	179

TABLE OF CONTENTS

CHAPTER 16 – THE DEVIL	188
CHAPTER 17 – THE TOWER	198
CHAPTER 18 – THE STAR	211
CHAPTER 19 – THE MOON	219
CHAPTER 20 – THE SUN	231
CHAPTER 21 – JUDGEMENT	242
CHAPTER 22 – THE WORLD	255
APPENDIX – TABLES	268
PAUL FOSTER CASE BOOK	271
WADE COLEMAN BOOKS	272

FOREWORD

In the early 1920s, Paul Foster Case copyrighted *An Introduction to the Study of the Tarot*. This work was the basis of a lesson series that Mr. Case wrote, *An Introduction to The Tarot*.

An *Introduction to the Tarot* was never copyrighted. *An Introduction to the study of the Tarot* copyright has expired, and the work is in the Public Domain.

Writing styles have changed in the last hundred or so years. Typically, Dr. Case would write paragraph sentences.

That is a sentence that would go on for three or four lines, using prepositional phrases and dependent clauses to illustrate a point, then clarify the point repeatedly by a series of examples, all within one sentence, with lots of commas and maybe a semicolon.

For the most part, my editing work was to break up his sentences by adding periods and removing double negatives.

Since Case's typewriter did not come with multiple font sets, he used transliterations of Hebrew letters. Therefore, they are replaced with Times New Roman Hebrew letters. I also added the symbols for the planets, astrological signs and the public domain black and white version of the Tarot Keys.

When possible, I changed pronouns to be gender-neutral. That is, changing "he" to "the individual," "we," or "you."

Additionally, I added an introduction to astrology which is fundamental to understanding yourself and others.

Also, some publishing software reads Hebrew from left to right. Normally, it's read right to left. I have no control over this feature, so please be aware that some Hebrew letters can be scrambled.

United States Copyright Office
Library of Congress · 101 Independence Avenue SE · Washington, DC 20559-6000 · www.copyright.gov

June 11, 2008

Our reference: 2008800241

This refers to your request of recent date.

Our search in the appropriate Copyright Office indexes and catalogs that include works cataloged from 1898 through May 16, 2008 under the names Builders of the Adytum; Paul Foster Case and School of Ageless Wisdom and the title (where available) AN INTRODUCTION TO THE TAROT disclosed no separate registration for a work identified under these names and this specific title.

During the course of this search, the following registrations were noted and are reported as of possible interest:

> AN INTRODUCTION TO THE STUDY OF THE TAROT;
> by Paul F. Case ... Registered in the name of Azoth Pub.
> Co., under A 573125 following publication May 20, 1920.

No search for possible renewal has been made since, in general, a work that was first published or copyrighted prior to January 1, 1923, would no longer be under copyright protection in the United States, insofar as any version published or copyrighted before this date is concerned. For further information, please see the enclosed Circular 22.

INTRODUCTION

The study of the Tarot is the most effective aid to human progress ever devised by the human mind. The Tarot is a wise and faithful counselor.

I have no intention of giving you a massive information dump about the Tarot. Instead, you will be given practical information on how you change your life for the better. In your Tarot studies, it doesn't matter if you have a long academic career or never finished high school.

Why?

Because the Tarot is already part of your flesh and blood. Through the study of the Tarot, you will gain, little by little, a considerable amount of esoteric knowledge. However, Tarot is your birthright. Its magic works whether you know all the details or none of them.

Tarot study is the training of the mind. The Tibetans and Hindus use mandalas to aid in concentration. The Western system uses Tarot symbolism, designed by the operation of man's mental activities. By keeping your consciousness fixed on a Tarot Key, you reach states of consciousness assumed by adepts.

We all want a greater measure of freedom and better health. If you persist with your Tarot practice, help is on the way. Some people experience dramatic changes when they start the study of Tarot. However, most people experience slow incremental improvements. The changes are so subtle that you don't notice until you reflect and reflect on your progress.

It may seem counter-intuitive, but progress is made by looking at pictures. Our minds use symbols. In many ways, they are more accurate than words. For example, consider a trip to the food store. For most people, it's easy enough to visualize the trip. Now, try to describe the excursion with words. It takes much more effort to use words than pictures.

Also, a dictionary is one of your most important tools as a practical magician. Make sure you understand the meaning of words before using them.

Tarot Practice

The first step is simple. Sit down in a comfortable chair or lay in your bed just before turning off the lights, and give yourself five minutes every day to look attentively at one of the twenty-two Tarot Keys.

The first day after you receive this lesson, look at the Key to get a general impression of the design during the five minutes. The next day, give a little more attention to the details. If you do see anything that seems to be important or that rouses your curiosity, make a note of it. Ask yourself, "What does this mean?" Sooner or later, you will get the right answer coming from inside.
Read your lesson at least twice a week. Most people must read their lesson three to five times before

understanding it thoroughly. In fact, after years of study, I'm always finding something new.

Read the lesson whenever you find a good opportunity. Don't work hard on it or anything else connected with your Tarot study. Above all, don't try to commit anything to memory.

A good time is in the morning after you finish dressing and before eating breakfast. I prefer night, so my Tarot practice is one of the last things I do before bed. What is important is selecting a time and sticking with it. Persistence ensures progress.

A word of caution. Do not devote more than five minutes at a time to the practice of looking at any one of the Tarot Keys. You are not yet an adept. Thus your brain is not at present adjusted to carrying the full load of an adept's consciousness. With time and practice, it will be. Make haste slowly.

More is not better. Three espresso shots are not better than one. It's just too much. Also, there is the law of diminishing returns. Some coal will feed a small fire. More coal will increase the heat. Too much will smother the flame.

Remember, every one of the Keys is a picture of some aspect of yourself. The subject matter of the Tarot series, from beginning to end, is always YOU. No matter what a picture may look like, as you first observe it, it is invariably a picture of YOU.

CHAPTER 1

Key 0 – The Fool – Uranus

Superficially, the Fool is a picture of a heedless, sky-gazing person just about to fall from a great height into a deep abyss. It corresponds to the proverbial wisdom concerning the folly of having one's head in the clouds. It has a valuable lesson even if you get no further than this with Key 0. One does risk danger when we are so engrossed with actual or metaphorical sky-gazing that we do not pay attention to our present situation. Therefore, the first lesson of Tarot is this: Don't project yourself so far into the future that you lose sight of where you are. Dreams, visions, and ideals have their proper place, but when we lose ourselves in the contemplation of airy nothings, we are unfit for dealing with the practical affairs of life.

All the Tarot Keys have two distinct levels of interpretation, the superficial significance seen at a glance. Also, the deeper inner meaning is brought to the surface of consciousness, without effort or strain, by attentively considering the Key.

At the deeper inner level of interpretation, the Fool is a picture of the power used in all our efforts to attain greater freedom. Various names have been given to this power, such as God, the Real Self, the Life-power, super-consciousness, etc. Names are only labels, some better and some worse than others.

Key 0 is the most perfect and complete aspect of yourself. It is the part of you that is above and beyond your external personality and beyond your thinking, conscious mind. Key 0 is a symbol of your very self, the whole of you, of which mind, body and everything entering into your seemingly separate personality are but parts.

Key 0 is a picture of the absolutely free and perfect Being, the animating principle and the core of your outer personality. In occult arithmetic, 0 does not mean nothingness. On the contrary, it stands for absolute Unity. The one reality which is before all beginnings. This is nothing we know directly. We cannot sense or define it. We cannot prove that it exists because it is beyond all our logic and reasoning, just as it is beyond every other conceivable limitation. Yet this One Life-Power is a real presence throughout the universe. Those who know bear witness that beyond knowledge and definitions of logic, there is possible a direct human experience of this Eternal Youth whose life runs through the creation and is the fount of vitality for all lesser lives.

The Fool stands close to the edge of a precipice. There is room for him to take another step forward. The esoteric tradition says this detail of the symbolism signifies an eternal truth. No matter how far the Life-power may advance, it can always take another step.

On a personal level, this means that you never come to the very limit of your possibilities. Sometimes you may wander into a blind alley, but even then, you can always retrace your steps and reach a place where further progress is possible.

There are profound metaphysical and philosophical reasons for selecting the title of Key 0. But one reason is obvious. Men of superior vision are always looked upon by their contemporaries as foolish. Consequently, every great prophet, inventor, and discoverer has been jeered at.

Not every tom-fool is superior to their associates. We must not fall into the error of those who look upon madmen as divinely inspired. Considering the advertisements on the religious page of any newspaper will be enough to persuade the thinking reader that psychosis is often mistaken for a prophecy.

The Number 0

The number 0 is shown in the lower-left corner of the card. The saying assigned to the number 0 on the Pattern on the Trestleboard is "All the Power that ever was or will be is here now." Key 0 symbolizes the power always at your disposal to further your growth and development. It is a symbol of the limitless, unconditioned Life-Power.

Zero looks like an egg, and an egg contains potencies for growth and development. A living body is formed inside the shell of an egg or womb and then hatched from it. The Cosmic Egg of the Life-power embodies everything in the universe. This egg or container is the Ring-Pass-Not.

The Hebrew Letter Aleph – א

The Hebrew letter in the lower right corner is Aleph (א). Aleph means bull or ox. Oxen are beasts of burden that plowed fields and hauled heavy loads. Therefore the letter Aleph represents the power to perform useful work. Furthermore, oxen represent the ability to adapt a natural force to the manifestation of our desires. Therefore Aleph is a symbol of cultural power. That is the development of intellectual and moral faculties through education.

Aleph is a natural force symbolizing creative energy and a vital principle in living creatures. This vital principle is shown in the upper right-hand corner of the card as the white sun. The Sun refers to the One Force. It is white to indicate that the Universal Radiant Energy is concentrated by and radiated from all the suns in the universe.

Aleph is one of the three mother letters. It is attributed to the element Air. Note that intelligence associated with Aleph is Scintillating (to emit sparks) or Fiery Intelligence. The element Air is the agency through which the power of the solar rays of our sun is carried to Earth. Additionally, the Air of the earth's atmosphere filters and steps down the energy so that it may be utilized by living creatures without causing harm. Fire creates and destroys. Air is a container and filter for the Fire element.

Practical Exercise

Look at the picture of the Fool for five minutes each day. Make no conscious effort to interpret the symbols.

If you do see anything that seems to be important, make a note of it and ask yourself, "What does this mean?" Sooner or later, you will get the right answer coming from within.

Purchase a loose-leaf notebook. However, please don't make any special endeavor to fill it. Instead, if you have An idea, jot it down on paper and put it in your notebook. Then, as you progress with this work, review your notes one or two evenings a week and add to them. Your interest will grow with your attention, and the longer you work with the Tarot Keys, the more they will intrigue you.

Read this week's lesson at least twice during the coming week and as often as necessary to ensure you understand it thoroughly. Read it whenever you find a good opportunity. Don't make hard work of it or anything else connected with your Tarot study. Above all, don't try to commit anything to memory.

The main practical use of Key 0 is to put you in touch with your inner sources of power. After you have looked at the picture for three consecutive days, you will find that you can summon it before the year mind's eye without any effort. Just think about it, and you will see it.

Thus you can hold your mind to this particular form whenever you desire. And you will find if you try it, that even a momentary glimpse of this gay traveler through the higher spaces will give you a lift. Try it whenever you are beset by a mood of depression. Don't try to suppress the mood. Just look at the Fool. Look at the actual picture if you have it handy. Glance at it mentally if you are away from home. Soon actual experience will convince you that there is always a positive reaction. This simple and easy practice will soon convince you that this picture has an almost magical potency. It's a sure antidote for depression.

Summary

The Fool is the Eternal Youth. He shows that the One Force never ages and is always at the height of its power. His attitude expresses confidence and joyful aspiration. It may seem like you are at the end of your resources. However, the Fool urges you to press on. Though you may be past mid-life, it knows itself to be forever young and knocks at the inner door of your mind, trying to let you know that in the very core of your being is a power that knows nothing of age or defeat or ill health. It is a power that transforms disaster into victory, lacks into abundance, and sorrow into joy.

The Fool is derived from the Latin follis meaning "bellows" or windbag. Thus the Fool symbolizes that which contains Air or Breath. This principle is also called Life-Breath. It is the Greek Pneuma, the Sanskrit Prana, and the Hebrew Ruach (רוח). Literally, these words mean "breath." Secondarily, they refer to the Spirit or all-pervading Life-energy.

The snowcapped mountains represent the abstract mathematical concepts behind all knowledge of Nature. The melting snow feeds the streams that make fertile valleys below.

The wreath around Fool's head symbolizes the vegetable kingdom and Victory. The wand is Will, the wallet Memory. The white rose represents purified desire.

The Fool's garments consist of a white undergarment and a black outer one lined with red. White is purity, truth, and wisdom. Black is ignorance and delusion. Red is passion, action, and desire.

The Fool's garment is held with a girdle, twelve ornaments, and seven shows. This girdle represents time. Because the Ancients measure time by the movement of the 7 planets through the 12 astrological signs.

The wheels which decorate the outer garment have 8 spokes. They symbolize the whirling motion by which the One Force manifests itself. The little dog symbolizes the intellect (Mercury), the reasoning mind. He is a faithful companion but must have a master.

⛢ – Uranus – The White Rose

Uranus is assigned to Key 0. In the Tarot, the white rose symbolizes Uranus and purified desire. Uranus is derived from the Greek word Ουρανος (Ouranos), meaning sky. Uranus has an axis tilt of slightly less than 90 degrees and rotates on its axis in a retrograde direction compared to the other planets. This makes Uranus the most "eccentric" planet in our solar system. Uranus' cyan color is due to methane in its atmosphere.

In astrology, Uranus brings liberation by shattering old patterns and conditions that are no longer useful. The challenge that Uranus brings to your life is to liberate your own true self. The process of liberation breaks old patterns and conditions that are no longer useful. As a trans-personal planet, Uranus has no concern about how your ego feels about these changes. Uranus' states of consciousness can manifest as divinely inspired knowledge and experiences and disruption and instability in your environment and personality. These experiences can have an electrical quality: sudden, unpredictable and intermittent.

CHAPTER 2

Key 1 – The Magician – Mercury

With this Key, the principle of contrast, which runs throughout the Tarot series, comes into operation. Every Key is, in some sense, the opposite and complementary of that which precedes it in the series. Also, the 22 Keys fall into 11 contrasting pairs – 0 and 1, 2 and 3, 4 and 5, etc.

The contrasts are obvious. Thus a Magician, or wise man, is in contrast to a Fool. The Fool stands on a barren height, and the Magician is in a garden. The Fool is preoccupied with his vision of a distant height, far beyond him across the abyss. The Magician is concerned with what happens in his immediate vicinity and looks down toward what is below him. The Fool's possessions are not in use, and he carries them in a wallet. The four implements of the Magician are spread before him on his table, and he has them ready at hand to use as the occasion arises.

Perhaps the most important detail of the picture of the Magician is the position of his hands. With the right hand, he lifts a wand upward toward the sky. The left-hand makes the universal gesture of attention, pointing with an extended forefinger toward the fertile earth at his feet.

The Magician symbolizes what psychology calls self-conscious awareness or the objective mind. This is the ordinary waking consciousness of human beings. It is the planning mind, the mind which comes to grips with our daily problems, and its basic function is attention.

Alert watchfulness is the key idea of the Magician. It is a picture or symbol of concentration. To your inner consciousness, this Key says:

Be alert. All the power you direct comes from a higher level. Make it your first concern to relate yourself to that source of power. Your place in the scheme of things is to act as an energy transformer. Force flows through you to whatever you give your full measure of attention. Nothing can withstand the mental force of an individual who has mastered the art of concentration. Yet concentration is as easy as pointing your finger. There is nothing difficult about concentration. Just watch, and keep at it. Then you can see through and into the things that constitute your environment instead of merely looking at them.

The garden of the Magician represents the subconscious field which is the source of the hidden powers we may direct in our quest for increasing freedom. These powers are symbolized by the lilies and roses. The white lilies stand for truth. The roses are symbols of human desires.

There are four lilies because all possible human knowledge falls naturally into four main categories symbolized by the four elements of the ancients, Fire, Water, Air and Earth.

There are five roses because every human desire relates to one of the five major senses. For all practical purposes, the fulfillment of any human desire includes bringing about conditions that may be experienced by one or more of our five senses. Desire is not evil. In fact, it is the motivation of evolution.

The Magician cultivates these flowers. That is to say, he improves them. By controlling their development, he takes them far beyond the conditions spontaneously provided by nature. The Magician is a transformer and transmuter of experience. Taking things as he finds them, he watches until he perceives the underlying principle at work. Then, by applying ingenuity, it makes new and different situations.

This is the true scientific method. The four implements on the Magicians table refer to this means employed by human self-consciousness in meeting and dealing with the human condition and environment.

The first means is symbolized by the wand. This is a pointer and is an extension of the pointing forefinger. The first step to solving any problem is to give it one's full attention. Every problem contains its own solution, which is perceived by attentive observation. This is the beginning of all science. Simple watching.

The cup symbolizes imagination. Observation collects experience. Imagination shapes it, as a cup shapes what is poured into it. So likewise, what we call "laws of nature" are simply man's collected experiences, related by acts of imagination.

The third means is action, symbolized by the sword. We may know a great deal, and we may have fine perceptions. But until we do something, nothing is changed. And our action invariably tears down something to replace it with something else. This is true of all effective action.

You can't build a house unless you cut down trees, cut stones, or take clay from a mud bank and make it into bricks. You can't paint a picture unless you remove the tubes' color. The statue never appears until the sculptor cuts away the stone, hiding the figure he imagined. Controlled and wisely directed destruction is the principal tool of civilization.

Finally, the finished product is represented by a coin because everything made by man's ingenuity has value. Please understand there is nothing wrong with having money. Poverty is no mark of spirituality.

Money is a wonderful invention and, when used rightly, a blessing. Nowhere does the Bible condemn money. What it does condemn is lust for money. Lust and love are poles apart. To love anything or anyone is to respect that thing or person and ensure proper regard for the proper use. He who lusts for things or persons is a stranger to love, seeking only selfish personal gratification and having no proper understanding of the object of his base desire.

Thus the coin is one of the most important symbols in this picture. Most of the sorrows of our day may be traced to two great errors, lust for money and contempt for it. Those who have proper respect for money understand it is one of the greatest human devices for promoting the general welfare.

Practical Instruction

Key 1 is the picture to use to develop your power of concentration, make you more alert, and evoke from your inner consciousness powers, enabling you to deal more satisfactorily with practical problems. Study this Key carefully, and it will help you to learn to concentrate, for its symbolism was created to that end.

Summary

The title refers to Man as the director of the force by which he transforms consciousness and reaches the stage known to occultists as Initiation.

The horizontal 8 or infinity sign above his head represents dominion, strength, and control.

The black hair bound with a white band symbolizes the limitation of ignorance by knowledge. The red rose is action and desire. The white undergarment, symbolizing wisdom, is encircled with the serpent of eternity. The table is the field of attention, which is the workbench of the Magician. The implements are the Wand, Cup, Sword, and Pentacle. They represent Fire, Water, Air, Earth; also Will, Imagination, Action and Physical Embodiment.

The Number 1

The number 1 is geometrically symbolized as a point. It means concentration, attention, and limiting the field of activity. This refers to the practice indispensable to all aspirants for truth. You cannot perform the Great Work until you have learned how to concentrate.

Geometrically the number 1 is a point. A point has a position but no dimensions. You can define a point in space perfectly. But that point does not occupy space. Thus the number 1 shares a property with the number 0. The zero is nothing that pervades throughout space. The point is nothing that only occupies one unique point in space.

The Hebrew Letter Beth - ב

The Hebrew letter Beth (ב) means "house." It suggests the sphere of human life and the family affairs of humanity which go on indoors. But the letter Aleph (א) on Key 0 means "ox" and has to do with what goes on in the field outside the special limitations of the human environment.

The first word in Genesis starts with Beth (בראשית). It is usually translated as "in the beginning," but it has many other meanings. Aleph is the primal fire before manifestation. Beth is the First Manifestation of the Primal Fire.

The Planet Mercury – ☿

Key 1 is attributed to Mercury. Mercury represents our mental functions and thought process. The ability to perceive and communicate. Mercury desires to express our perceptions and intelligence through skill or speech. Therefore, Mercury is attributed to communication, academic, and intellectual matters. Mercury is the messenger archetype that transmits messages between the Soul (the Sun) and the personality (Ascendant).

Essential Dignities of the Planets

Each planet has particular astrological signs that it operates for better or worse.

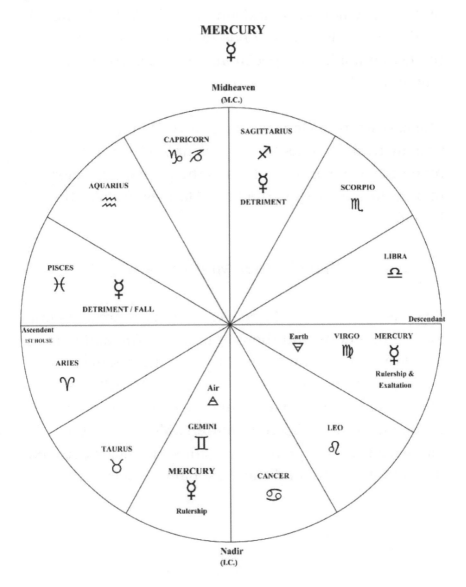

Mercury Rules Virgo

A planet in Rulership or Domicile is at home. This is where the planet is most comfortable. Mercury rules Virgo, a Mutable Earth sign. In Virgo, Mercury communicates logically and critically. However, Mercury in Virgo can also be skeptical and sometimes negative because the well-developed mind can see all the ways a plan can go wrong. Sometimes Mercury's over-attention to detail can hinder the perception of the big picture.

Mercury also rules Gemini. Mercury communicates fluently, quickly, cleverly, intelligently, and sometimes superficially in this sign. In this sign, Mercury's curious mind expresses his perceptions immediately. Mercury in Gemini expresses his nervous energy through talking, writing, or other forms of manual/mental dexterity.

Mercury in Sagittarius – Detriment

Mercury is good with details. But in Sagittarius, a Fire sign ruled by Jupiter, Mercury's thinking can be clouded by over-generalizations and idealistic aspirations.

Mercury in Pisces – Fall / Detriment

Pisces is a Water sign also ruled by Jupiter. In Pisces, Mercury is sensitive, idealistic, imaginative and evasive. In Pisces, the powers of reason can be confused by daydreaming and self-deception.

Summary

A planet in Rulership or Domicile is at home. In rulership, planets express their function positively.

A planet in Detriment is in a sign contrary to its nature. The planet feels uncomfortable and lacks confidence. The planet is in conflict with itself.

A planet in Exaltation is at the pinnacle of his/her rank. In exaltation, the planet operates at its best.

A planet in its Fall is like someone involved in something inappropriate for their skill set.

Please, don't be discouraged by the amount of information. As you continue these lessons, these terms will become clearer through repetition.

CHAPTER 3

Key 2 – The High Priestess – The Moon

This is a picture of a calm, seated woman. In the colored deck, The High Priestess is predominately blue, the coldest of colors. She contrasts with the warm red, which dominates the color scheme of the Magician. The High Priestess is passive, receptive, and, by ancient meanings of the title, virginal.

The High Priestess's robe is made of Water. This is the universal water, Mind Stuff or subconsciousness. Water flows and conforms itself perfectly to its container. When you pour water into a vase, it perfectly duplicates its form. Thus the High Priestess is associated with memory because memory is a record or duplication of an event but is not that event.

The High Priestess's book or scroll is also associated with memory and past records. In prehistoric times, these records were transmitted orally, from mouth to ear. Thus they were committed to memory. The written word is simply an artificial memory.

Memory is the basic power of subconsciousness. The High Priestess sums up all that is needed to use memory in her symbolism. Not that using the Key will enable us to recall everything. It is just as important to be able to forget as to remember. Several mental diseases are characterized by the too-perfect recollection of past experiences.

Notice that we say nothing about improving memory itself. Careful tests have demonstrated the fact that subconsciousness retains everything. It records the trivial, useless, and significant parts of our experience.

No clear impression escapes being written in the scroll of the High Priestess. Memory is perfect. It cannot be improved.

By intelligent use of Key 2, we can develop our power of recollection, our ability to duplicate past experiences, and our skill in using the law whereby mental images are grouped together in our subconscious filing system.

Such skill presupposes concentration and attention, the mental activities associated with the Magician. Much of what is called faulty memory is want of attention. If the camera is badly focused or not even pointed at what is going on, the pictures will either be dim, or the film will be blank.

Hence, the first requirement for better recollection is to be alive and alert to what is happening around us. We must be "here," or we forget.

The High Priestess is perfectly quiet, perfectly passive. This is the first requirement for good recollection. Strain to remember something, and it refuses to come to the surface of your mind. Just sit still and relax, and you will find the needed information, no matter what it may be, rising easily to the surface, provided that the first impression is clear and sharply defined. For blurred, hazy images, we know no remedy except a change from careless inattentiveness to deliberate determination to be fully alive to what happens during every waking moment.

Artificial mnemonic systems are of little or no value except for mental tricks. Instead, give your subconsciousness a chance by giving it clear images as you go along, and its automatic filing system will soon put your mental house in order.

We say automatic because the laws of recall work automatically. We make them useless by inattention. We interfere with their operation when we struggle and strain to remember. But if we know what they are and let them do their work, we can recall anything we require.

Key 2 pictures all the laws of memory. The two pillars are alike in shape because we naturally group images like one another. Yet these pillars are opposite in color because the 2nd law of association is that of contrast. Think of light, and you also think of darkness. Mutt's lanky length calls up the squat, chubby form of Jeff. So similarity and contrast are both symbolized by the pillars because these two laws always act together.

A 3rd law is recency. Other things being equal, we recall easiest what we have most recently experienced. The latest news, the funny story we heard this afternoon, the interesting display in some window we just passed an hour ago, all these we recall without effort. The High Priestess does not have to turn her scroll to read what she has just recorded.

The 4th law is repetition which is directly related to the number 2 but has several other representations in the various details of the design. Anything frequently repeated is easy to recall. Give the casual glance most of us grant to a new acquaintance, and a second meeting may call forth no flash of recollection. See an individual day after day, and you can recognize them at a distance.

The 5th law is intensity. We remember our first experiences because they received full voluntary attention. Childhood is, therefore, more vivid than yesterday, but if we learn to renew our youth – and the secret of this is in the Keys of Tarot – we shall once more live deeply and fully and have vivid memories instead of hazy impressions.

Tarot is one of the best mnemonic systems. By the time you finish this course, you will have 22 sharply defined mental pictures, each associated with a number.

Think of a picture, and you will see the number printed on the Key. Likewise, think of a number, and the picture will flash instantly before your mind's eye. No effort is needed. Numbers and pictures go naturally together.

Since the associations are not arbitrary, making the Tarot the basis for a wonderful aid to recollection is possible.

Suppose, for instance, you have five things you must do without fail tomorrow. It takes no time, and little effort, to link these activities, utilizing visual images, with the first five Tarot Keys.

Begin by making a list. Get the things you have to do in proper order. Suppose the first is to see your physician. You might imagine the word DOCTOR written in large white letters on Fool's wallet. The more fantastic the association, the easier the recollection. But the image must be directly related to what you wish to recall.

If the second thing you must do is to attend to some correspondence, you might imagine a big pen lying on the Magician's table with the rest of his implements. Or perhaps the image of a pile of letters on the same table may suggest itself. It does not matter what, so long as the image directly relates to what you desire to remember. As a rule, the first picture that comes is best.

Don't jump ahead of this course to acquire the mnemonic system we have just described. For now, use Tarot for recollection training, nothing other than your 5-minute session with the High Priestess.

Remember, Tarot speaks a pictorial language you know subconsciously. You do not have to learn it. You have only to let yourself be spoken to through your eyes. The High Priestess will do wonders in making your subconsciousness realize that you expect it to put its extraordinary power of associating ideas at your disposal.

Practical Instruction

Whenever you want to recall something, sit down quietly for a few moments and bring before your mind's eye the picture of Key 2 to recall what you want to remember. Be as relaxed as you can. Don't cast about in your mind for the desired piece of information. Instead, look mentally at this image of the Perfect Recorder of all experiences. You'll be amazed at the result.

Summary

The universal substance has been called by some modern scientists "mind-stuff." However, occultists have known for ages that the universe is really made up of mental energy. This primordial substance, known to the Hindus as Prakriti, has always been symbolized by Water and a Virgin.

The symbolism of the stone cube has many meanings. The first is the Hebrew word for stone is eben (אבן). It's an esoteric word representing Union, Life, and Wisdom.

The teaching (Tora) of the wise is a fountain of life, turning a man from the snares of death. – Proverbs 13:14.

The Hebrew Letter Gimel - ג

The Hebrew letter Gimel means "camel" and suggests travel, commerce, and carrying news from one place to another. As a hieroglyph or pictograph, Gimel looks like a foot, suggesting travel or a person in motion. The meaning implied is, *walk, gather* and *carry*. It also implies a group because the feet bring people together.

As an aside, in astrology, the feet are assigned to Pisces and Key 18, the Moon. And the Moon as a planet is assigned to Key 2, The High Priestess.

Each Hebrew letter can be spelled in full. For example, Gimel's (גמל) letter name is spelled right to the left, and the three letters are Gimel (ג), Mem (מ) and Lamed (ל). These letters spell camel. However, by pronouncing the same letters differently *g'mal*, the meaning changes to:

1. Requital: something given in return, compensation, or retaliation.

2. Recompense: make amends to (someone) for loss or harm suffered; compensate.

3. Remuneration: money paid for work or service.

Notice the definition implies people. So one person is being compensated or receiving, and the other is giving. But a third thing is implied, that which is given.

Each letter is also a number in Hebrew, Phoenician, and Greek languages. Gimel is equal to the number 3.

Key 2 is the High Priestess. However, the letter printed on the lower right-hand corner is Gimel and numerically 3.

The Number 2

In the number 2, we have a contrast to the singleness of 1, in the doubling or duplication which 2 implies. Combined with the ideas which are suggested by camel, 2 gives us the notion of the two extremes of a journey, its beginning and end; of the two necessary to strike the bargains made in commerce; of the two who are concerned with news, those who hear and those who tell.

Geometrically, the number 2 is a line. A line is a length (straight or curved) without breadth or thickness, the trace of a moving point.

The Moon

☽

The Moon is the only "planet" which orbits the Earth. It spends one half its orbit between the Earth and Sun and the other half between the Earth and Pluto. Thus it serves as a link between the outer and inner planets. Through the law of correspondence, one of the Moon's symbolic functions in our birth charts is as an agent which connects the power of Spirit (Sun) to matter (Saturn).

Hence the Moon is receptive, a provider of life, and has the power to build forms. On a physical level, our mothers embody these qualities. The potency of Spirit comes through our mothers as she gives birth to the form and substance of our physical vehicles. This is why the Moon represents the mother.

The Moon represents our feeling and how we nurture ourselves to emotionally integrate our experiences. The lunar force is responsible for our emotional growth, maturity, and personal happiness.

The Moon is also involved with the subconscious process. It is our "unconscious reactive habit patterns," which are often concealed from conscious view. So, for example, when we are under stress, we instinctively do those things that nurture us to make us feel emotionally safe and secure.

The Moon's Essential Dignities

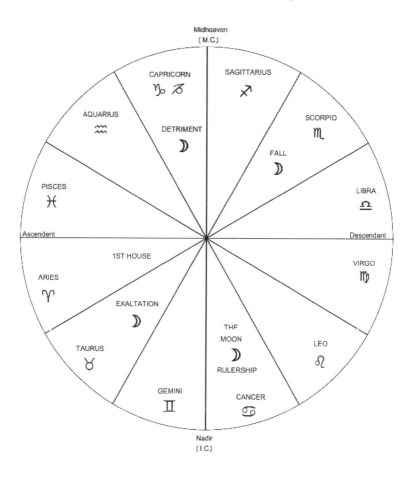

The Moon Rules Cancer

Emotionally Tenacious

In Cancer, the Moon is emotionally tenacious. The Moon Rules Cancer, a cardinal Water sign. In Cancer, the Moon is nurturing and protective of others and values its home life. Key 7, the Chariot, is attributed to Cancer. In this Key, it is evident that Moon is security-conscious.

Moon is in its Detriment in Capricorn

Emotionally Reserved

Capricorn is ruled by Saturn. Therefore the Moon is reserved and cautious in expressing its feelings.

The Moon is Exalted in Taurus

Emotionally Stable

The Moon rules on the etheric plane. Taurus is a fixed earth sign and provides the etheric and physical substance for the lunar influences to work.

The Moon exaltation confers the ability to steady the feelings and generate the vital energy needed to give ideas physical manifestation. In Taurus, the Moon is determined to obtain practical results in any project they undertake.

The Moon is in its Fall in Scorpio

Emotionally Possessive

Scorpio, a fixed Water sign, is ruled by Mars. In Scorpio, the Moon seeks emotional security and stability by trying to possess the object of their desire. However, loved ones are not possessions; this nurturing style doesn't work well.

Also, the Moon in Scorpio is loyal and unafraid of adversities and challenges. That's their bread and butter.

Planets in Detriment and Fall

A word about planets in their Fall and Detriment. Depending on how you use the energy, it can be an asset.

For example, a friend told me a story about raising her son. She has a Moon in Capricorn. She got tired of forcing her son out of bed every morning and bought him an alarm clock.

On the first day, he turns it off and oversleeps. As a result, the young man misses the bus and walks to school in the rain.

She gets a call from the school administration stating her son is late and soaking wet. She responded, "Well, he's not a sugar plum, so he won't melt."

It was his fault he missed the bus, so he walked to school in the rain and got detention for being late. After that, the young man was never late to school again.

A Moon in Cancer would have driven the boy to school, and he would have learned nothing except when I make a mistake, my mom bails me out. However, with a mother with a Moon in Capricorn, he learns the consequences of his actions. Moon in Cancer invented the saying "tough love."

I know this is a lot of information and can be overwhelming. So I'll try to keep the rest of the chapters shorter.

The Hebrew Letters and Values

Key	Title	Hebrew			Pictogram	#
0	The Fool	Aleph	א	F	Ox	1
1	The Magician	Beth	ב	i	house	2
2	The Moon	Gimel	ג	n	foot	3
3	The High Priestess	Daleth	ד	a	door	4
4	The Emperor	Heh	ה	l	arms raised	5
5	The Hierophant	Vav	ו		nail or peg	6
6	The Lovers	Zain	ז		sword, sickle	7
7	The Chariot	Cheth	ח		fence	8
8	Strength	Teth	ט		Serpent, coil	9
9	The Hermit	Yod	י		hand	10
10	Wheel of Fortune	Kaph	כ	ך	open palm of the hand	20
11	Justice	Lamed	ל		shepherd's staff	30
12	Hanged Man	Mem	מ	ם	water	40
13	Death	Nun	נ	ן	seed sprout	50
14	Temperance	Samekh	ס		thorn	60
15	The Devil	Ayin	ע		an eye	70
16	The Tower	Peh	פ	ף	a mouth	80
17	The Star	Tzaddi	צ	ץ	net, snare	90
18	The Moon	Qoph	ק		coil, circuit	100
19	The Sun	Resh	ר		the head	200
20	Judgment	Shin	ש		teeth, fangs	300
21	The World	Tau	ת		Mark	400

The final letters are used when they come at the end of the word. For example, Aleph (א) spelled in full is (אלף).

Aleph (א), Lamed (ל), and final Peh (ף). Notice that Peh is in its final form at the end of the word.

CHAPTER 4

Key 3 – The Empress – Venus

Key 3 symbolism is predominantly feminine and outdoors. In the Tarot, the outdoors symbolizes self-conscious activity, while indoors is subconsciousness. Also, male figures are symbols of self-consciousness, and females are subconsciousness. Therefore Key 3, the Empress, is self-conscious subconsciousness or Creative Imagination. In this operation of subconsciousness, there is an apparent accretion of materials around a vital center. This is true in mental as in physical creation.

Imagination is the mind's ability to make new combinations from the store of remembered experiences. Therefore, the Empress is associated with Daleth (ד), meaning door, because creative imagination is the entrance to a new life and new worlds.

The symbols in Key 3, the Empress's pregnant womb, wheat, trees, green grass, river and waterfall, suggest growth and fruitfulness. This is a symbol of the magician's union with the High Priestess. That is to say, thoughtful observation (Key 1) of our environment brings about the subconscious activity (Key 2) that links different ideas into new and novel forms (Key 3).

The stream and waterfall symbolize the stream of consciousness. It flows from the robe of the High Priestess, like all the streams pictured in the Tarot. The water falling into the pool represents the positive and negative potencies of the Life-Force. These potencies are also symbolized by the scepter of the Empress.

Key 0, the Fool, symbolizes the limitless Life-power that assumes all forms. What specific forms it takes are the ones where you place your attention. What you make the object of your attention is what you become sooner or later. Focus on images of misery, poverty, and weakness; their physical embodiments will become part of your surroundings. Your body is part of your environment, and if your personal Magician works the black, destructive transformations resulting from fear and apprehension, your house of life will be built in strict agreement with those ill-drawn plans.

Change the patterns by attending to their opposites, and creative imagination, symbolized by the Empress, will begin to build you a new life and impress the conditions of your environment with new ideas.

Look closely at your problem, and you will discover the answers to the problem. Moreover, you will be enriched by numberless clear realizations of how things really are instead of being burdened with useless repetitions of how things look.

The combining and associative power of subconsciousness will continually make you aware of new images. As a result, your mind will be as fertile as the Empress' garden, and you will reap a wonderful harvest of ideas.

The yoke of the true Law of Life is easy. Success is assured for those who are persistent upon the Path until it leads them out of the fogs of appearance into the clear illumination of the true realization.

Eliphas Levi has this to say about imagination.

"The understanding and the will of man are incalculable instruments in their power and capacity. But the will and understanding have an auxiliary instrument which is too little understood. I speak of the imagination.

"Imagination is the eye of the soul, and it is therein that forms are delineated and preserved; by its means, we behold the reflections of the invisible world. It is the mirror of visions and the apparatus of magical life. Thereby we cure diseases and modify the seasons... this faculty exalts the will and gives it power over the universal agent.

"Imagination determines the form of the child in its mother's womb. It gives wings to contagion and points to the weapons of warfare. Are you exposed in a battle? Believe yourself as invulnerable as Achilles, and you will be so, says Paracelsus. Fear attracts bullets, and courage turns them back on their path.

"There is no invisible world. There are merely various degrees in the perfection of organs. The body is the rude representation and the perishable coating of the soul. Spiritual and corporeal are words that express degrees in the tenuity and density of substance. What we call the imagination in man is the inherent faculty of the soul to assimilate to itself the images and reflections contained in the living light... In this only, the man of genius differs from the dreamer and the madman in that his creations are analogous to truth, while those of madmen and dreamers are lost reflections and wandering images. Thus for the sage to imagine is to see, and for the magician to speak is to create. The seer knows with an absolute knowledge that the things he imagines are true, and experience invariably confirms his visions."

Powers like Levi describes may seem far beyond your present attainments. Nevertheless, no adept walks the earth today (and there are many now living in all parts of the world) who was not once beset by the same delusions and miseries you may suffer now.

The rich fertility, the calm peace and happiness, and the ability to order all things aright, pictured in Key 3, are not something you can acquire. On the contrary, they are inalienable possessions, which is your right and duty to put into use.

Let your contemplation of this Key begin the process of renewal for you. Like this happy, radiant woman, your inner life forms the new image and likeness of a new personality. It does not matter what your past has been. Your future is yours to create. To build the meaning of this Tarot Key into your flesh and blood is to set in motion forces that, at first, work almost imperceptibly below the surface and will inevitably bring to pass fulfilments far beyond the best of your present expectations.

Practical Instruction

Look at Key 3, The Empress, five minutes a day. As you look, summon whatever knowledge you may have gathered about the tremendous power of that silent potency, LIGHT, to aid you in understanding that mere looking is actually directed use of the same radiant energy, which is the basic substance of the whole physical universe.

There is nothing you know that is not made of light. You employ no force or power that is not a transformation of that same illimitable radiance. No matter how much you utilize, there is always room for more. Infinity is inexhaustible.

The practice is simple. Too simple for some types of minds who think nothing is effective unless it is full of sound and fury. Yet we may remember the old saying, "The world belongs to the silent ones." The potent forces of the universe work noiselessly and without friction, like an engine in perfect order. Our faulty machinery requires tremendous temperatures (indicative of tremendous waste) to accomplish what even the lowliest of weeds performs without any appreciable heat output. And our bodies are far, far higher in the scale of evolution than those of plants. Already men and women walk this earth like the gods they really are. The Tarot Keys are their gift to us that by using this most potent instrument, we may become members of that increasing host, the Great Companions who tread the Path leading to the heights of liberation.

The Hebrew Letter Daleth - ד

In Key 3, we return home from our journey on the camel (Gimel, ג) to the door (Daleth, ד) of the house (Beth, ב). Daleth, in Hebrew, means "door." A door is a means of entrance and exit, a passageway from within to without.

The door is a feminine symbol representing birth, reproduction, and the entry of life into manifestation. Daleth is the womb, the door of personal life. It opens to receive the seed and closes to retain the germ during gestation. Then, it opens again to send the new life into the world. This activity also occurs on planes above the physical.

The Number 3

Geometrically, the number 3 is a triangle. A triangle is 3 points connected by a surface between them. The number one is a point. The number two is a line. The number three is a plane. In geometry, a plane is any flat, two-dimensional surface. A two-dimensional surface has length and width but no depth. Therefore, to fully enter the world of name and form has to wait for the number 4.

When the masculine principle is combined with the feminine principle, the results are always the same on any plane, growth and development of something new.

Venus

♀

Venus, Goddess of Love, holds court in interpersonal relationships. Through our communion and closeness with others, we establish values and ideals to create comfort and harmony in our relationships and environment. Through relationships, Venus expresses its internal experiences as emotions and affections.

This is why Venus represents our emotions. We get emotions as a result of our external contacts. Out of our relationships spring joy, pain, or sensuality.

Our hearts are moved by spiritual forces. However, Mars is motivated by more ego-based physical forces and desires. Together, Venus and Mars combine to create a spectrum of love.

When Venus is betrayed or neglected, we lose heart; we alienate ourselves by forbidding intimacy, relationship, and love.

Venus Dignities

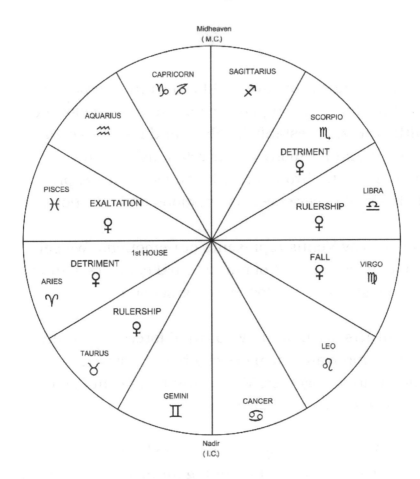

Venus Rules Taurus

Venus in Taurus expresses affection physically, warmly, steadily, and possessively. Loyalty. Gives from inner resources. Appreciates physical sensations: sight, sound, smell, taste, and touch. Enjoys contact with nature. Values material comfort and also beautiful and practical physical objects.

Venus is in Detriment in Scorpio

Expresses affection intensely, obsessively, with extreme, consuming feelings. An urge for pleasure is colored by compulsive desires, depth, and passionate emotions. Needs can be hindered by an inclination to secrecy and trust issues. Needs to penetrate deeply into a relationship with intense emotional power to feel close to another.

Venus Rules Libra

Expresses affection lightly, considerately, charmingly, and harmoniously. Give-and-take with others is colored by balance, fairness, and gentleness. Peace, tranquility, and harmony are needed to feel comfort and pleasure. Needs to develop relationships based on equal sharing and cooperation to express one's emotions.

Venus is in Detriment in Aries

Expresses affection directly, impulsively, and enthusiastically. Emotionally directed toward new experiences, especially enjoys the first stages of relationships. However, the need to feel close to another can be thwarted by strong self-assertive, demanding qualities; intimacy, therefore, sometimes is difficult to achieve. Values individuality, initiative, and independence in self and others.

Venus Is Exalted in Pisces

Expresses affection sensitively, kindly, compassionately, and sympathetically. Empathy. Romantic Idealism. Active Imagination. Musical talent. Lack of discrimination can hamper forming of solid relationships.

Venus in its Fall in Virgo

Venus in Virgo expresses affection matter-of-factly, modestly, helpfully, and timidly. A need to serve and be useful for emotional satisfaction. Finds pleasure in attention to detail and analytical mental activity. A need for logic and practicality to feel comfortable and harmonious. Over-helpfulness and petty emotional criticisms of one's natural reserve can interfere with emotional expression. Venus in Virgo is looking for the "perfect" love.

The Daily Rabbit Hole – Shibboleth

An Excursion into Gematria

The symbolism of the Tarot is subtle and rich. For example, in Key 3, consider the rise of fifty wheat by the fall of water.

In Hebrew, an ear of corn or grain is *She.ba'let* (שבלת). The same letters with different pronunciations are *Shibboleth*. It means *current* (of a river), *eddy*, or *vortex*.

And so the symbolism of a rise of wheat/corn/grain by a fall of water is *Shibboleth*. This word is used once in the Bible, Judges 12:5-6.

The Gileadites captured the fords of the Jordan leading to Ephraim, and whenever a survivor of Ephraim said, "Let me cross over," the men of Gilead asked him, "Are you an Ephraimite?" If he replied, "No," they said, "All right, say 'Shibboleth.'" If he said "Sibboleth" because he could not pronounce the word correctly, they seized him and killed him at the fords of the Jordan. Forty-two thousand Ephraimites were killed at that time.

What does this mean?

It's probably a lot of things. Using gematria, I looked up the words in the Bible using *The Interlinear NIV Hebrew-English Old Testament* by Kohlenberger.

Sibboleth	And he said	Shibboleth
סבלת	ויאמר	שבלת
492	257	732

732 – Shibboleth – The Potential

L'ven (לבן) white, whiteness; white of the eye, silver coin; semen.

Reshah (רישא) chavurah (וראה), the white head, a title of Kether (variant spelling, see 736).

T"va.shal (תבשל) You shall cook, boil. Exodus 23:19.

257 – And He Said – The Word

Na.aur (נאור) enlightened; illumined, splendid, glorious; enlightened, cultured.

Tzadek (צדק) av.nay (אבני) Just weights. Leviticus 19:36.

492 – Sibboleth – The Result

Tsore (צור) olahmim (עולמים) Everlasting Rock. Everlasting Strength. Isaiah 26:4.

Beth (בת) Melek (מלך) The King's Daughter. Psalm 45:13: "The king's daughter is all glorious within (the palace): her clothing is of wrought gold."

Zibeth (צבת) handful. Name of the stone of the Philosophers, which Lamech says contains "the first elements, and the final colors of minerals, or spirit, soul, and body, joined into one."

Conclusion

Make your own conclusions, and entertain ideas. Venus has an *active imagination* - a valuable tool when using gematria.

The Rabbit Hole Inside the Rabbit Hole

If you take the time to count the shafts of wheat on Key 3, the Empress, there are fifty (50).

The Hebrew letter Nun (נ) is fifty (50). Nun means "seed" and "to sprout." It is the letter on Key 13, Death.

In Ancient Egypt, the mound (*Benben* Stone) that arose from the primordial waters of **Nun** is where creation took place. In Key 3, the Empress, the wheat springs from the well-watered soil. They are colored brown because they are of the Earth.

I know, last lesson I said I'll keep the lessons shorter. But this lesson concerns Venus and creative imagination, so I get a free pass.

CHAPTER 5

Key 4 – The Emperor – Aries

The Emperor comes after the Empress. A man cannot be the master of his household until his mate has children. Fatherhood is a consequence of what the mother brings into the world.

Key 4, a monarch ruling all his kingdom, is a true portrait of your own SELF. He is a man of war, clad in armor and wearing the purple of royalty. Like the High Priestess, he sits on a cube (a symbol of truth). On the cube is a ram's head corresponding to Aries, the first sign of the zodiac.

Regulation and supervision are implied by the symbols in Key 4. Note that supervision is *overseeing*. Thus the function of sight is attributed to Heh (ה) and the Emperor. Sight is chief among our senses. Through it, we regulate our lives and our world. The quality of our vision determines the course of our progress.

In medical astrology, Aries rules the head, the cerebrum (responsible for thought and action), the eyes, the face, and the upper jaw. Therefore Aries and the Emperor are attributed to vision and reason because reason is "insight" or mental vision. Thus the fundamental meaning of Key 4 is reason. It is how we govern our lives and daily activities.

Unless we imagine, we do not really see. Physical vision demands more than the correct optical functioning of the eyes and brain centers. Occasionally an individual born blind receives their sight, but after this occurs, it takes months to learn to see. For the newly sighted, there is no difference in appearance between a globe and a disk. People walking toward him seem to grow as they approach. Until imagination based on other senses enables him to supplement what his eyes report, they have no true vision of the world on which their eyes have opened.

We have all passed through this experience, but because we learned these lessons in infancy, we have forgotten that we had to learn to see as surely as we learned to walk. The mind is the true seer. The eyes are only its instruments.

The control the Emperor directs is not the imposition of our desires on the world. We never force nature to obey us. On the contrary, she serves us at a price. We must see things as they are. Definitions must square with fact. Reasoning must be a development of accurate observation. Then imagination will be true, and vision will materialize as a fact.

The Tarot study's most valuable result is that human consciousness is enriched and transformed by it so that we learn to see the true world hidden behind the veil of superficial appearances. Nature is always for man, never against him.

Nature is never against humanity, but it has its own agenda. The Egyptian Text of the Bronzebook says:

> "Forget not that life has, but one purpose, one end, and one objective, and that is the awakening of the souls of men. All things on Earth conform to that end. Earth without perplexities and

problems, its struggle and strife, its inequalities and injustices, would never develop the soul to meet its destiny. This is the answer to the riddle of ages. If all were right with the Earth, there would be nothing for man to do; as it is, there is sufficient to occupy him throughout his generations. When man is perfect, its purpose will be fulfilled, and then Earth, too, will be perfect." – Book of Morals and Precepts 4:13.

The mountains represent abstract reason. They are colored red for the fiery activity of Mars and Aries.

His armor is for protection and is colored violet or purple. Violet is Jupiter's color, dignified by Triplicity in Fire signs (Aries, Leo, and Sagittarius). Therefore, the truth (Jupiter and Law) protects the Emperor.

The Emperor's scepter is a modification of the symbol for the planet Venus (♀). Note the "T" section of the scepter has a symbol of the Sun (☉) on top. That's because the Sun is exalted in Aries.

The "T" is also a symbol of Tav (ת) and Saturn (♄). In Aries, Saturn is put to good use by Emperor.

The globe is a symbol of dominion. On the globe is the Tav or Saturn symbol shown upside down. Saturn is a symbol of limitation and restriction. The reversal of Tav indicates that the powers associated with Key 4 can overcome obstacles and limitations.

Practical Instruction

The symbols of Key 4 suggest to your subconsciousness that now you are a master of your external circumstances and conditions. No matter what appearances to the contrary, the truth is that your personal world, just as it presents itself, is the world you have made for yourself. You may not like it, but you made it. And because you made it, you can remold it, nearer to the heart's desire.

The false world of the ignorant does not actually exist. It has no more reality than a nightmare. Yet we have all experienced bad dreams and know how dreadfully acute their terrors are. Use Key 4 to wake you from the dream that you are a slave to circumstance, from the delusion that anything you have thought, said or done in days gone by can rob you of your heritage of freedom. No system confers this freedom. It comes from our inner consciousness.

The true vision and correct definition destroy before they build. They who remold worlds must begin by shattering them to bits. Destruction is the foundation of existence. This is one of the lessons from the strong Mars quality of Key 4.

The Hebrew Letter Heh - ה

The earliest pictograph of the letter Heh was a man with raised arms. This suggests Look! See, reveal.

In Ancient Egypt, Heh is the god of eternity. Heh, as a hieroglyph is numerically, one million. He holds a pair of notched palm branches which signify 'year.'

Image Courtesy of Wikimedia Commons

In Hebrew, the letter *Heh* is a definite article. It means "the." For example, in Hebrew, *bet* (בית) means house. By adding Heh in front, it is *ha-bet* (הבית), which means "the house." Therefore the letter Heh makes things definite. It singles out objects that are similar to each other. This letter symbols mental activity where we single out particular things and differentiate them from others more or less like them.

The Number 4

Four relates to the classifying activity of self-consciousness (Key 1, The Magician), induced by the response of the subconscious (Key 2, The Empress) to create mental images (Key 3, The Empress). Finally, these mental images are arranged by classifying activity in reason (Key 4, The Emperor).

The number 4 symbolizes the square and is associated with manifestation. Eliphas Levi says, "... This number [4] produces the cross and square in geometry. All that exists, whether good or evil, light or darkness, exists and is revealed by the tetrad, (it is) the unity of construction, solidity, and measure."

Thus the words associated with the number 4 are: *order, system, regulation, management, supervision, control, authority, command, dominance, classify,* and *reason.*

♈ Aries – I am

Aries is impulsive, energetic, and pioneering as a cardinal fire sign. They like to lead. However, the desire to lead is different from the ability to lead. Excessive self-assertiveness is Aries failing. Aries tend to "make their own rules," sometimes getting them into trouble.

Aries develops a sense of selfhood, structure, and limits through conflict. Hence the key phrase describing the underlying Arian motivation is **I am**.

When Aries have the foresight to plan, they make good leaders. These individuals work best where they can express their own ideas and put them into execution and where they can direct the activities of other people.

Aries Attributes

Element: Fire. Identity. Inspirational. Intuitive. Spirit and Will. Activity. Inspired. Excitable.

Quality: Cardinal. Action. Initiative. Dynamic. Outgoing radiant force.

Desire. Initiative. Forceful, courageous and impulsive. Single-handedly taking charge towards self-definition and spontaneity. Single pointed release of energy to new experience. Aries to seeks to discover their identity through action.

+   Aggressive, competitive, outgoing, energetic, courageous, spirited, confident

-   Selfish, impulsive, rude, bold, audacious, too daring, crude, too direct

Planetary Dignities in Aries

Mars Rules Aries

Asserts self competitively, dynamically, and impatiently. The single-pointed release of physical energy directed toward a new experience. A flair for starting new businesses and/or mechanical ingenuity. Faces obstacles directly, but recklessness can impede success. Sexual drive and physical energy are expressed impulsively, powerfully, and confidently.

Sun is Exalted Aries

Radiates forceful, confident vitality. Enterprising and ambitious. Competitive. The forceful assertion of individuality is necessary for self-expression. Energetic leadership. Explorer, pioneer, the first to begin an adventure; quickly grasp essentials. Maybe insensitive to other people's needs but rarely holds a grudge.

Venus is in Detriment in Aries

Expresses affection directly, impulsively, and enthusiastically. Emotionally tastes directed toward new experiences, especially enjoys the first stages of relationships. Strong self-assertive, demanding qualities can thwart the need to feel close to another; therefore, intimacy is sometimes difficult to achieve. Values individuality, initiative, and independence in self and others.

Saturn is in its Fall in Aries

Aries is Cardinal Fire that likes to lead. Aries's motto is, "Let's do something, even if it's wrong." They learn from their mistakes and move on. However, Saturn Aries needs to think before it acts. They need exercise to release pent-up impatience and irritation.

CHAPTER 6

Key 5 – The Hierophant – Taurus

The Hierophant is associated with hearing. Because in medical astrology, Taurus governs the throat, neck, lower jaw, ears, and hearing.

However, physical hearing is not the only meaning of Key 5. It also symbolizes interior hearing, whereby we may know the Voice of the True Self, pictured as the Hierophant. Therefore the meaning of Key 5 is "Intuition," in the sense of inside tuition or interior teaching.

Notice that Key 5 follows Key 4. Genuine intuition is not a substitute for reason. It is a logical consequence of good reasoning. Intuition does not teach the lazy-minded. Whenever a person tells you he does not need to study because intuition tells him all he needs to know, they're usually a liar or deceived themself. The Inner Teacher wastes no time in fruitless endeavors to instruct the incompetent who will not take the trouble to observe (Key 1), to remember (Key 2), to imagine (Key 3), and to reason (Key 4).

Intuition is your true Teacher, coming from your own Inner Self. That self is represented by the Hierophant. In this connection, we must caution you that true interior hearing is not the negative, lower psychic type of clairaudience. The difference is readily distinguished by the quality of what is heard. Intuition is above reason but never contrary to it, and it never urges you to do something unethical or selfish.

The Emperor and the Hierophant are the same. The difference between them is in their spheres of operation. In Key 4, the emphasis is on the objective, external world from where we gather experience. Key 5 emphasizes the inner realm, whence an individual gains wisdom and knowledge of the external world. There are not two worlds. Actually, they are just the outside and the inside of one world. The one is not more real nor truer than the other. The outer world is devoid of meaning, apart from the inner one. The wisdom of the Inner world is dead if it is not put to use and service in the realm outside. Either realm, taken by itself, is incomplete and, to that extent, false.

The Voice vs. voices

In these lessons, we use a capital V when writing this "Voice." It must be distinguished from the "voices" of other minds or discarnate entities on the astral plane. We do not discount the virtue of internal communication with other entities, whether they be minds of incarnate men and women or minds of the discarnate. Yet none of these, however wise may be their counsel, is the Voice. This Voice speaks where there is none to speak. It is the Voice of the One Self, and the knowledge and wisdom it imparts have no tinge of human fallibility.

In the 32 Paths of Wisdom, Key 5 and Vav are assigned to the "The Triumphant and Eternal Intelligence." Triumphant because its counsel always helps us overcome obstacles, avoid danger, and transform seemingly adverse circumstances into friendly cooperation with our efforts. Eternal, because this council is always based on eternal principles. Never is it merely a thing of the moment.

To open our inner ears is not enough. There are enemies and friends of man on the astral plane. Mischief-makers delight in perplexing and confusing those who listen to their suggestions. Yet they always betray themselves by certain characteristics.

First, they flatter subtly and in the ways, one is most susceptible. They flatter by revealing "mysteries" reserved for the rest of the world. One of their commonest tricks is to reveal details of past incarnations. For those of grosser wits, they say, "Once you were Cleopatra, or Napoleon," or some other prominent figure of the past. To others, they find the way to domination by revelations of supposed former incarnations, not particularly striking in themselves, yet seeming to render plausible the idea that one's present shortcomings are a natural outcome of past experiences.

These revelations always aim to establish confidence in those giving the communications. Their sources of information are tremendous. They who live in the astral plane, and use the astral senses, can read our lives from the cradle onward. Names, dates, and even our private thoughts and feelings are engraved on the scroll of the High Priestess. Thus the accuracy of any spirit's revelation of your past is not a guarantee of his good faith. Some entities are well-meaning and benevolent, but a man does not become a Master simply by shedding his physical envelope. Many well-meaning people give bad advice and keep giving it when they get on the "other side."

For example, dying does not turn someone into a financial wizard. Discarnate entities don't have bodies. Therefore, they have no concerns about food, water, shelter or sleep. Therefore, their advice on these subjects is usually not practical.

Stop your ears whenever you hear a voice that demands you obey its dictates. The Voice never demands, flatters, and does anything to increase your sense of personal self-importance. Furthermore, every principle it announces may be checked by reason. Sometimes the revelations of the Voice go beyond reason and ordinary experience. Yet in no single instance do they run counter to reason, and they meet the tests of investigation.

Symbols

The *two ministers* kneeled before their Teacher wearing garments embroidered with the same flowers in the magician's garden. They represent personal acquisitions of knowledge (lilies) and the development and cultivation of desires (roses).

The *crossed keys* have a bell design on the wards (the part of the key that goes into the lock). This symbolizes that sound vibration and hearing are necessary to unlock the gates of your Inner Temple.

The crossed keys are colored gold for the Sun and silver for the Moon. These are the traditional keys to heaven (gold) and hell (silver). According to C. C. Zain, the gold key is astrology, and the silver key is the Tarot.

The *pillars* represent the Law of Polarity or the interplay of the pairs of opposites. Their capitals show a ball and socket pattern and an acorn surrounded by oak leaves. The oak is considered a cosmic storehouse of wisdom embodied within its towering strength.

Practical Instruction

Look up the image of the Hierophant whenever you are confronted with a problem to which you cannot find a solution. Then, practice the listening attitude of mind after doing all you can in observing, remembering, imagining and reasoning. The Voice never speaks loud, and you will fail to hear it until you have learned to silence the clamor of your thinking or to talk to yourself.

The fundamental practice is to be still when you wish the counsel of the Voice. Stop racking your brains when a seemingly insoluble problem confronts you. The harder you try, the less likely you are to hear the answer. In Key 5, there is a strong element of what is pictured in the High Priestess and the same need for quiet calmness.

Every great principle and eternal truth is already part of the wisdom of your true self. Intuition is a form of recollection. It brings up treasures of wisdom buried deep in humanity's subconsciousness. It also brings down new treasures from the super-consciousness awareness. And always, the price of these revelations is silence. You cannot listen if you are talking to yourself.

Take your problem to the One Teacher, and listen to what he may have to say. This does not mean that you will hear an audible voice. However, if you are consistent in your practice, you will really hear the Voice, and after having had this experience once, you will never mistake the Voice for any of the "voices."

The Hebrew Letter Vav - ו

"The Vav is a vertical line representing a pillar or a man standing upright. The world stands on pillars. The pillars, a symbol of support, hold creation together." [Ginsburg, 1995, p. 97]

The Hebrew letter Vau (ו) means *nail* or *hook* and is the conjunction "and." For example, in Hebrew, Eben (אבן) means stone. By adding a Heh (ה) at the beginning of the word, it becomes ha-eben (האבן) and means "the stone."

By adding a Vav (ו), the word becomes va-ha-eben (והאבן), meaning "and the stone."

The Number 5

The number 5 sits in the middle of the numerals from 1 to 9. Occupying this central place suggests *intervention*, *mediation*, and *adjustment*; hence *justice*, *accommodation*, and *reconciliation*. A mediator serves as a link between two opposing groups. In Tarot, Key 5 links four pairs of pictures--1 and 9, 2 and 8, 3 and 7, and 4 and 6.

Taurus – I have

♉

As a fixed earth sign, Taurus seeks to establish security and stability in the physical plane of human activity. Venus rules Taurus and pursues its need for security and stability by fulfilling its desires.

Taurus Attributes

Asserts self steadily, retentively, conservatively, stubbornly. Strong actions are directed toward consolidation, productivity, and enjoyment of simple pleasures. Often a creative and/or artistic flair. Initiative and drive are colored by material concerns, possessiveness, and sometimes slowness and laziness. Achievement of desires may be thwarted by complacency and satisfaction with things as they are. Physical energy and sexual drive are influenced by a deep appreciation of life's physical senses and natural rhythms.

Stabilizing influence. Slow and persistent. Establishing self-reliance through constant and steady efforts. Self-substantiation. The depth of appreciation is related to immediate, physical sensations. The image of a tree, stable, immovable, deep roots. Enjoys the physical environment. Motivated by material insecurity. Possessiveness and practicality. Inertia and determination. Materialistic. Sense oriented.

+ Practical, steadfast, cautious, pragmatic. The viewpoint is "show me." Reliable, persistent, steady.

- Possessive, jealous, plodding, slow to change, self-indulgent, hedonistic.

Planetary Dignities of Taurus

Venus Rules Taurus

Taurus is a Fixed *Earth* Sign ruled by Venus. Venus rules both Libra and Taurus. In Libra, a Cardinal Air sign, Venus likes art and beauty. Therefore Venus in Libra wears high heels because they make her *look attractive*. Venus in Taurus wears sandals or goes barefoot because it *feels better*.

Venus in Taurus is loyal and expresses her affections physically, warmly, and steadily. Venus deeply appreciates physical sensations: sight, sound, smell, taste, and touch; she enjoys contact with nature. In addition, she values material comfort, luxury and beautiful physical objects.

As do all fixed signs, Venus in Taurus tends to be possessive. A need to give of one's affection can be hindered by emotional stinginess, possessiveness, or reluctance to release feelings or lose control.

Mars in its Detriment in Taurus

Venus rules Taurus, and this influence tends to make Mars a bit lazy. However, a leisurely pace is not the same thing as idleness. Mars in Taurus is a slow starter but often goes farther than most - Tortoise (Mars in Taurus) and the Hare (Mars in Aries).

Persistence is their virtue. Physical efficiency and physical comfort are inseparable. If Taurus is comfortable at work, he tends to work more efficiently but not faster. The easiest way to anger a Taurus is to rush them.

Ordinarily, Taurus is good-natured. And though they are slow to anger, their rage is fearfully destructive when aroused.

The Moon Is Exalted in Taurus

The Moon in Taurus creates a powerful etheric vehicle, producing healthy bodies and great stamina. It provides the ability to steady feelings and generate the vital energy needed to give ideas physical manifestation. The Moon in Taurus is determined to obtain practical results in any project they undertake.

CHAPTER 7

Key 6 – The Lovers – Gemini

The main lesson of this Key 6 is important to all who wish to make the best use of their powers. In simple terms, it is this: Super-consciousness (the angel) sheds its influence impartially upon both self-consciousness (the man) and subconsciousness (the woman). Despite the ancient philosophical terminology which makes subconsciousness seem what Orientals call the "inferior" nature, while self-consciousness is termed the "superior," these two are co-equal.

That is, they are fundamentally so, but when these two aspects of the personal nature of man come under the "curse" mentioned in the allegory of the Fall, the woman becomes subject to her husband. Therefore, her restoration to her rightful place of equality is one of the great practical works of Ageless Wisdom.

Despite the miseries St. Paul's interpretation of the allegory of the Fall has visited on womankind, there is a great truth. Subconsciousness is always amenable to suggestion and, unless rightly directed by self-consciousness, falls easily under the sway of the appearances and illusions having their source in physical sensation.

These appearances and illusions are pictured in Key 6 as the serpent coiled around the tree behind the woman. The tree has five fruits representing the physical senses, which seems attractive to those who yield to its temptations. It is not that the life of sensation is evil, but all that humanity knows by sensation consists of pairs of opposites – good and evil, as the Bible allegory describes. However, physical sensation and their pair of opposites fall short of providing us with all the information we need to succeed in life.

As the allegory of the Fall puts it, Adam and Eve were perfectly happy as long as they obeyed the Lord. But when they listened to the serpent, they found themselves in trouble. The "Lord" is the personification of super-consciousness, pictured in Key 6 as the angel. As long as the personal life is under the direction of Super-consciousness (the angel), all goes well. However, all goes wrong when the connection with super-consciousness is broken by mistaken endeavors to plan one's life by the reports of physical sensation.

Remember, the "Lord" is not an outside ruler who imposes his will on human beings. There is no such ruler. The true Self is, in one sense, superior to any human being and has an existence far beyond the limits of any human personality. However, that same Self is the innermost reality at the core of every human life. Depending on that as your source, guidance, and sustenance, one's life is regulated and arranged from a level superior to the best self-consciousness that can reason and superior to the best subconsciousness that can imagine.

Key 6 pictures the situation and the logical consequence of the steps depicted in the Tarot Keys preceding it. When the Magician is consciously related to what is above him, every pattern he makes (symbolized by the arrangement of implements on his table) is good. From this, it follows that the record on the scroll of the High Priestess is clear and definite, and then the mental imagery produced by subconsciousness is the good wheat in the Empress' Garden.

Under such conditions, the Emperor is not a petty tyrant but is completely identified with the One Self so that, to all intents and purposes, "God" acts directly through the personality. The Emperor, though the Magician in another guise, is also one with the Fool and is therefore pictured with a single eye and a white beard. This symbolism subtly references occult representations of the Ancient of Days. His clear vision is supplemented, and its true significance is made manifest by the Voice of the Hierophant. Thus, the happy state of balanced and harmonious relationship pictured by the Lovers is brought about.

The two human figures in Key 6 are nude because they conceal nothing from each other. Just as a man and woman who love have no shame or secrets from one another, the two aspects of personal human consciousness, which relate to super-consciousness, have no concealments.

In Key 16, The Tower, we shall see a picture of the destruction of false knowledge. In this Key, the two human figures are completely clothed. The average human being is in disguise. His words and face say one thing to his contemporaries. However, his inner thoughts say something very different. He is "putting on an act" that deludes himself and becomes a victim of his pretenses.

This sort of play-acting is what is meant by the word "hypocrisy." The woes Jesus pronounced on hypocrites must not be misunderstood as punishments inflicted upon sinners. The miseries these people suffer are the logical consequences of the conflicts in their minds. Being full of guile, they cannot be members of spiritual Israel. Guile is evidence of our own self-deception. But he who deliberately surrenders his personal life to a super-conscious direction becomes the immediate agent of the One Life.

Key 6 gives your subconsciousness a very definite suggestion with far-reaching consequences. It says:

> "The two aspects of human personality are different but equal. The one is no 'better' than the other. Each has its own special powers and a special field of operation. It is not the office of self-consciousness to tyrannize over subconsciousness like an old-fashioned husband. Neither is it the part of subconsciousness to take charge. The two must have no concealments. They must leave one another free to carry out their particular types of activity. Self-consciousness has the job of observing the objective world and gathering accurate data. Subconsciousness has the job of acting as the connecting link between self-consciousness and super-consciousness. Our contact with the Voice of the Hierophant is established through subconsciousness. It is through subconscious channels that we arrive at an understanding of significance. Through subconsciousness, new ideas and new mental imagery come into manifestation."

Practical Instruction

Look at Key 6 five minutes a day. Absorb as much of its meaning as you can. Then use your ingenuity to frame a special message to your subconsciousness. Let the words be your own, but let the central idea be this:

"From now on, subconsciousness, you are no longer amenable to suggestions by me at the level of my self-consciousness unless those suggestions are confirmed by super-consciousness. You are free from errors of the Past."

Remember, the deliberate, reasoned surrender of all personal domination over your subconsciousness is not the same as turning over your personal life to the whims of subconsciousness.

The results of your practice may not appear immediately, yet in the long run, you will find that all conflicts between your subconsciousness and your self-consciousness are cleared up. You will find yourself experiencing, day after day, the wonderful and beneficent results of super-conscious guidance.

This does not mean that you will never make any mistakes. Your self-conscious mind has limits. It is fallible. However, if the subconscious is waiting for confirmation from super-consciousness, the consequences of our superficial errors are easy to overcome and correct.

Zain – ז – The Sword

Nails (Vav, ו) fasten things together. Swords (Zain, ז) cut them apart. Thus there is a contrast between the letter printed on the Lovers and that assigned to the Hierophant. Vav is a symbol of union. Zain, the sword, is division.

A sword is an instrument of division and cleavage. The intellect also divides by noticing the differences between similar objects. Thus, the Sword symbolizes *discrimination* and the active principle of overcoming inimical entities or forces.

"…it is no coincidence that the letter Zain symbolizes sustenance and armament. The two concepts are related to each other. The letter Zain is shaped like a spear, indicating that man's sustenance is obtained by his struggle." – *The Wisdom of the Hebrew Alphabet.*

As a symbol, it is represented by the spear, dart, arrow, that which tends to an end: As a grammatical sign, it is the demonstrative sign, abstract image of the link which unites things." – *Hebrew Tongue Restored*, d'Olivet, 1976, p. 339.

Symbols

The Sun symbolizes enlightenment and the ONE FORCE, which is differentiated into pairs of opposites.

The angel represents super-consciousness, the man is self-consciousness, and the woman is subconsciousness. The clouds symbolize that super-consciousness is partly hidden from us at our present stage of development.

The mountain symbolizes attainment. They are colored purple or violet, Jupiter's color dignified by Triplicity in Air signs.

The tree of 12 flames behind the man represents the zodiac signs. Behind the woman is the tree of good and evil with 5 fruits for the 5 senses. Also, the five senses enable us to discriminate between one thing and another.

The Number 6

Six is the first "perfect number." This is because the sum of the prime numbers that make up 6 (1, 2 and 3) equals the multiplication of the same prime numbers.

1 + 2 + 3 = 6

1 x 2 x 3 = 6

Thus the ideas associated with the number six are reciprocation; interchange; correlation; response; coordination; cooperation, correspondence; harmony; concord; equilibration; symmetry and, thus, Beauty.

Gemini – I Think

♊

As a mutable air sign, Gemini is flexible and mentally adaptable. Gemini has a fluid versatility and natural curiosity about everything, like a young child discovering the wonders of their universe for the first time. If taken to an extreme, this quality can make Gemini superficial or scattered and fails to penetrate the surface of things.

Gemini Attributes

The concrete mind. Changeability. Duality. Restlessness. Literary and academic matters. Diversification. Ambiguous and curious. Continually interacting to gather enough information about its options. Perception and verbalization of all connections. Learning and teaching about social and intellectual realms. Motivated by intellectual and personal insecurity.

+ Curious. Hungry to learn and teach. Neutral. Adaptable. Social. Excitable. Versatile. Friendly. Lively. Witty.

- Restless. Unreliable. Scattered. Superficial.

Mercury Rules Gemini

Mercury in Gemini communicates fluently, quickly, cleverly, and intelligently. Mercury learns through establishing connections among people and ideas. A changeable curious mind expresses itself through friendly interactions and endless questions. High nervous energy levels are expressed through talking, writing, or other forms of manual/mental dexterity.

The North Node is Exalted in Gemini

In astronomy, the ascending node (North Node) is where the Moon crosses the ecliptic from south to north, and the descending node (South Node) crosses from north to south. The North Node is also known as the Dragon's Head and is considered fortunate or helpful.

The North Node in Gemini increases versatility, adaptability and mental agility. Benefits come from relatives and friends because of an optimistic perspective toward life.

The North Node in Gemini indicates victory after much anxiety and trouble. It symbolizes success and luck, which often comes only when everything seems lost. The North Node in Gemini is a symbol that *progress* can be made.

Jupiter is in Detriment in Gemini

Jupiter is good at looking at the big picture but not so good with the details. In Gemini, Jupiter can be overwhelmed with too much information. As a result, optimism is hindered by excessive thinking and worrying.

CHAPTER 8

Key 7 – The Chariot – Cancer

The scene in Key 7 presents many contrasts between the Lovers. Key 6 shows everything in a state of nature. The human figures are nude. They stand in open country, and their surroundings show no trace of human invention or handicraft. Key 7 multiplies the fence idea in various ways. In the background is a city surrounded by a stone wall. At the foot of the wall is a river. It is another defense to protect the inhabitants of the town. In the foreground, the chariot is a portable fence, and the rider wears armor that protects his body – especially his chest – against injury. Furthermore, to confirm the attribution to this Key of the sign Cancer, each shoulder of the rider bears a lunar crescent, and the Moon is the ruler of Cancer.

The face in the crescent at the left of the picture is forbidding and severe, while that on the other side wears a smiling, benign expression. This contrast is also shown in the two sphinxes that crouch before the car.

In Key 6, the two human figures stand apart despite receiving equal influences from the angel above. In Key 7, the rider's body joins the two lunar masks, and the two sphinxes are a team united in drawing the car. Thus Key 7 represents the unification and reconciliation of opposites. In Key 6, the stress is on the antithesis presented by the male and female figures. In Key 7, the idea of synthesis is prominent in every design part. Furthermore, this synthesis is achieved by human agency.

Psychologically, one of the meanings of Key 6 is right discrimination. But all the meanings of Key 7 involve synthesizing the various principles we have been considering up to this point. The synthesis is Will.

Ageless Wisdom unequivocally declares that free will is part of the makeup of every human being. Yet it is equally emphatic in its denial that there is any such thing as a separate power of volition peculiar to each human being. The only WILL in the universe is what exoteric theology calls "the will of God." But the esoteric doctrine is at sharp variance from the exoteric fancy that any man has a will of his own which he can oppose to the will of God. When any person supposes to have personal free will is suffering from a fundamental delusion.

In Key 7, the river symbolizes the esoteric doctrine of the will. It flows into the picture from outside and flows out again. In like manner, the very real power we feel inside ourselves as that which we exercise in acts of volition is not something having its source in our personality. It is something that flows through the field of personality.

The word vehicle is a synonym for chariot and is a clue to the esoteric function of human personality and will. Persons are instruments and agencies of the One-Life. Persons originate neither themselves nor their actions.

Please do not mistake our meaning. We repeat that Ageless Wisdom insists that Free Will is a true component in the makeup of each human being. Our denial of the personal element in free will is no denying man's essentially free power of volition. We are saying that the person is not the man – that the person is, as the very word person indicates, only a mask, agency, or vehicle through which spiritual humanity finds expression.

In Tarot, the human is the Fool, the Magician, the High Priestess, the Empress, the Emperor, the Hierophant, the Angel over the Lovers, and the Rider in the Chariot.

The person is symbolized by the garments of the Fool and by his wand and wallet. The Magician's implements, robes, and garden flowers represent the person. So it is throughout the series. Those elements related to personality are always subordinate – as the scroll of the High Priestess and the ministers kneeling before the Hierophant. If this is kept in mind, the inner meaning of Tarot will be more clearly revealed to you as you continue using it. The whole purpose of these Keys may be summed up as Self-revelation, as psychological training enabling you to live in intimate contact with the SELF and experience the beneficent consequences of this union.

Receptivity is the personal attitude that is indicated by Key 7. The main purpose of a chariot is to contain its rider. The main purpose of a fence is to contain the field it surrounds. The field is not physically separate from the land outside. The wall or fence is an artificial means of setting aside a portion of land for a specific use.

Similarly, human persons are like fenced fields. They are not really separate. The walls which seem to set us apart from our neighbors are artificial. Little children are usually unaware of them. Education and training have erected most of those high barriers that hem us in.

Because our education begins at a time before our earliest memories, we fail to realize that much of our seeming isolation is due to habits and attitudes imposed on us by our parents and other elders. They who become highly proficient in occult training must break down many artificial fences.

When they succeed, they regain the use of powers that are humanity's rightful heritage. We often insist that occult training will not give you new powers. Rather it will restore to you powers that you did exercise in early childhood but have now forgotten.

For example, little children are in telepathic communication with their parents. Every observant mother has innumerable evidence of this – but observant mothers are few. Most of them fail to grasp the significance of what is indicated by much of the behavior of infants.

In fact, most of the higher powers we supposed to be unusual seem to be so because our faulty training has stifled them. We can all communicate with other people, irrespective of the physical spaces that seem to separate us. We are omnipresent because the true Humanity at the heart of every human personality is God.

That true Human is the real source of free will, and when we come to understand this fully and deeply, we shall know how to bring into effective action powers which now seem far beyond our present limitations.

Cheth – ח – A Fence

The letter Cheth means a *field*, *fence* or *palisade* (a line of steep lofty cliffs usually along a river). This implies enclosure. This field can be the manifested universe, but it's the personality in humans. The One-Self sets aside a particular point in space and time to cultivate the personal ego.

Symbols

Key 7, The Chariot, represents the Conquest of Illusion. The Charioteer is the Inner Self. The sphinxes are the senses. The invisible reins represent the Mind. The Chariot is the body, which is drawn by the sphinxes.

The idea of enclosure and protection are suggested in the symbolism. For example, the sign Cancer attributed to Key 7 means Crab, an enclosed crustacean. The Chariot, the armor of the rider, the wall in the background, the battlements and towers are all symbols of the same idea.

The starry canopy represents the celestial forces whose descent into matter is the cause of all manifestations. The Hindu lingam-yoni symbolizes the union of opposite forces on the shield in front of the Chariot. Above the shield is a winged globe.

The globe is the Sun. The wings represent the alchemical element of Air, which carries the power of solar rays. The wheels represent Jupiter, rotation or cyclic activity. The scepter, a combined crescent and figure 8 symbolize the combined powers represented by the Magician and the High Priestess.

The rider is the Holy Guardian Angel, a symbol of the power to establish harmony out of chaos. It is a power of adaptation and adjustment. Equilibrium results from equilibration; the concrete application of the laws of symmetry and reciprocation brings poise, rest, art, and victory.

Practical Instruction

As you look at Key 7, remember that your personality is an instrument or vehicle for expressing the same limitless Willpower which marks out specific fields of expression for the One Life.

Begin your exercise by sitting still; use every device in that stillness. Imagination suggests that your personality is maintained by a stream of vibrating influences flowing into and out of it. Try to see that all power is yours at every moment.

Let no sense of effort attend this exercise. You do not generate the current. Therefore, though some people shout over the telephone, they do not follow their bad example.

The Number 7

A 7-pointed star cannot be constructed accurately with a compass and straight edge. It requires human thought, trial, and error before accurately constructing one. Thus the number 7 is associated with mastery, conquest, peace, safety, and security.

Cancer – I Feel

♋

The symbol for Cancer is the Crab, which carries its dwelling (a house, a symbol for self-consciousness) upon its back. The slow-moving crab lives part of its life on land (the physical plane) and also in the sea (the emotional plane).

Cancer is very receptive and sensitive to the feeling of others, which can make them react at the whim of their feeling and emotions. Cancer is invested in the creation of a home and family. Cancer feels insecure when forced on unfamiliar ground.

Cancer Attributes

Element: Water. Feelings. Emotional. Soul. Psychic. Empathic.

Quality: Cardinal. Action. Initiative. Dynamic. Outgoing force.

The home and family. Receptivity. Sensitivity and feelings. Maternal instincts. Action and initiative applied to emotional and soul concerns. Emotionally engaged. Tenacious with feelings. Instinctive nurturing and protective empathy. Protective of whatever it identifies with emotionally. Clannish.

+   Empathetic. Nurturing. Tenacious. Family oriented. Mystical. The trust of the world that the earth senses do not perceive. Connection with the archetypal values. Worldwise. Strong need to be creative, to flow and give birth to something.

-   Clingy. Moody. Defensive. Needy. Guilt/manipulative. A need to be needed.

Moon Rules Cancer

The Moon in Cancer reacts with sensitivity and protectiveness (toward self and others). The Moon feels secure when nurturing and being nurtured by others. A natural sense of timing and ability to tune in to the intuitions and emotional subtleties. Sensitive to the reactions of others.

Saturn is in Detriment in Cancer

Saturn rules Cancer's opposite sign, Capricorn, which is practical, ordered and structured. In Cancer, a Cardinal Water sign, Saturn faces wet and fluid uncertainty. Saturn in Cancer is challenged to respect emotions without blocking them until they spill out uncontrolled.

Jupiter is Exalted in Cancer

Cancer rules the home and family relationships. Jupiter also rules social conduct based on mutual goodwill among the members of society. With Jupiter in Cancer, the individual can expand his concept of family to include a larger social whole. Jupiter can be emotionally sympathetic to people around them and treat them as family members.

Mars is in its Fall in Cancer

Mars is the warrior who fights. He fights for sex, survival and just for fun. You supply the justification, and Mars supplies the sword.

Mars in Cancer must feel connected with one's roots and traditions to understand one's desires and direction in life. Initiative and willpower can be hindered by moodiness and cautious self-protection, but they are capable of fearless action to support loved ones.

Cancer is home and family. Therefore, Mars in Cancer can represent conflict at home. Conflict (Mars) with mother (Moon).

Mars in Cancer is dignified by *Triplicity* in Water signs. In Water signs, Mars considers other people's feelings before reacting and is rewarded with good male (Mars) friends.

CHAPTER 9

Key 8 – Strength – Leo

Key 8 takes us back to nature, away from the associations of human artifice connected with Key 7. The letter attributed to this picture is Teth (ט), which looks like a serpent. Thus there is an echo in Key 8 of what we have already seen in Key 6, where a woman and a serpent were part of the design.

Teth – ט – The Serpent or Coiled Basket

Teth (ט) represents a snake or serpent and symbolizes immortality and eternity. It is a symbol of the Great Magical Agent. The motion of the Great Magical Agent is serpentine. It is wavy, undulating, and like a spiral. Teth is derived from the Phoenician alphabet, which represents a *coiled* basket made of woven fiber.

The serpent is associated with evil, temptation, and antagonism to God or man. This is because of man's ignorant misuse of the serpent power. Because it has a wavy motion, spiral, or coiling force, it is typified by the serpent. Yet this same force is the instrument of man's liberation when used correctly.

Key 8 shows two principal symbols of this force – the snake (the tail of the Lion) and the lion. This is the Bible's Adversary and Redeemer. Exoteric theology believes the Redeemer and Adversary are irreconcilable antagonists. However, the truth is the same force that the wise employ to attain freedom from bondage is also the same force, when ill-directed, causes all human misery.

The serpent symbolizes a dangerous animal with a deadly poison, killing human beings quickly and painfully with the bite. Thus, all the exoteric religions naturally identify the snake with the devil.

Some individuals believe they are protected against misfortune by denying the existence of the Adversary. Victory is empty unless there is a real antagonist to overcome. Even a game of bridge would be meaningless unless there were opposing sides. And when we deal with the various problems of human existence, nothing is sillier than to believe we may escape danger by pretending it does not exist. Problems are never solved by refusing to face them.

Neither are they solved by vain attempts to destroy their causes. On the contrary, like poisonous snakes or weeds, the causes of evil are to be overcome, and to overcome an adversary is to make him an ally.

Thus the message of Key 8 is of particular importance to all lovers of freedom and justice at this present crisis in the history of civilization. It tells us that the enemy, though dangerous as a deadly serpent or a roaring lion, can be transformed into a powerful ally.

In Key 6, the serpent of temptation is shown coiled around the tree behind Eve. In Key 8, the same force is pictured as a red lion, but now the woman tames the beast, and she opens his mouth and gives the lion speech. When we understand the seemingly adverse power, we can tame it and make it the instrument to express and realize our aspirations. Step by step, the progress of human science brings the dumb, brute forces of nature under the control of human thought. For millenniums, lightning was only a type of swift death, and thunder was mistaken for the voice of an angry God. Now the same lightning carries the human voice in a flash to every part of the world. This subtle force is symbolized by the letter Teth and the lion in Key 8, Strength.

The method to bring this force under control and direction is simple. First, it is the law that subconsciousness is always and completely amenable to control by suggestions originating at the level of self-consciousness. In Key 8, this is intimated by the woman wearing a white robe similar to that of the Magician and having the same horizontal figure 8 over her head, shown in Key 1.

Key 8, Strength, is assigned the astrological sign Leo, ruled by the Sun. Wherever there is a physical form, it is identical to the radiant energy streaming from innumerable suns throughout the universe. It is stellar radiance or astral light.

This radiant force streams from our sun to provide energy for our entire world system. Out of this energy, all the complex things surrounding us are built.

Every form taken by this energy in our environment is a form of life and is, therefore, a form of consciousness. Ageless Wisdom says everything is alive. Inorganic, as well as organic forms, are built from this vital electricity.

Wherever there is life, there is some degree of consciousness. The latent consciousness of minerals and vegetables appears to be unconsciousness or subconsciousness. Recall that subconsciousness is all the levels of awareness below that of human awareness of a Self or Ego. And every level of consciousness below that of self-consciousness responds automatically to suggestions at the self-consciousness level. Through thought and imagination, we may impress our will upon our environment.

We adapt to our environment directly and indirectly by imagining and using tools. Machines are thought forms materialized by human imagination. For example, a chair is a projection into a physical manifestation of a man's thought of sitting. When an individual imagines truly, by following the steps outlined in Tarot by Keys 0 to 7, nature responds to bring a greater measure of freedom.

Yet we have seen that machines can enslave as well as liberate us. However, it is not the machines, but our thoughts about them, which constitute whatever bondage we may suffer.

Some men and women worldwide have progressed beyond this indirect control of the astral light. Instead, they use a variety of instruments for their works of power. The tarot is one such instrument. This Introduction to Tarot will lead the persevering students to a point where they can produce positive changes in their environment.

Because the inner meaning of Key 8, Strength, leads to some of the most important practical secrets of occultism, we are cautious in explaining this picture. Yet one point we do wish to emphasize. The lion is led by a chain of roses, and the roses mean just what they mean in Keys 1 and 3. They are symbols of desire, and this is a cultivated desire. In Key 8, they are woven into a chain. What is meant is that the subconscious levels of the activity of the cosmic radiant energy are to be controlled by trained, systematic, coherent use of related desires.

Practical Instruction

Looking at Key 8 will evoke from your inner consciousness a realization of the truth that you are now in touch with an inexhaustible and always available source of power. This picture tells you the truth about your relation to all the forces which constitute your environment. It tells you that what ignorance fears and dreads as a malignant adversary is really your most potent ally. As you use it, it will evoke a mood of courage and confidence. For beginners, this is the most important practical application of Key 8. Try it, and you will find that whenever you are depressed or a little bit frightened at some appearance in your personal world, a glimpse of this picture will raise your spirits and dispel your fears.

Kundalini

This card has a very profound esoteric significance. It represents the great cosmic force that Madame Blavatsky called *Fohat*. In the human organism, this force is called *Kundalini*, the Serpent-Power. Some systems attempt to tell unwary students how to awaken the sleeping Kundalini. They are too often successful, and their misguided efforts result in human wrecks and derelicts. People are driven to madness and obsession. The fact is that Kundalini is a real force and is as powerful in destruction as it is in integration. *Every person automatically receives the instruction he needs to awaken Kundalini when the time comes for that awakening.* In the meantime, listen to no one who tells you he can help you unfold powers by setting the serpent force in action. Such practices are the most dangerous known to man.

The proper way to prepare yourself for the time when you can do such a thing safely is to learn how to control your body, mind, and emotions. When you have done this, you will know what your next step is to be. Kundalini is not a force to be feared. You really use it every day of your life. But you use it naturally and without giving it conscious attention. Even in its latent state, it is the force behind your activities. It is automatically controlled by subconsciousness. Subconsciousness is the woman in Key 8, who controls the lion completely. Because Tarot works by giving suggestions to subconsciousness, it works automatically towards the expansion of consciousness that makes for greater control over continually increasing powers of personality.

The Secret of All Spiritual Activities

Each one of the letters of the Hebrew alphabet is assigned to one of the 32 Paths of Wisdom. These few pages of text are found in the *Sepher Yetzirah*. For example, the letter Teth is assigned, *The Secret of Spiritual Activities*.

"[The 19th Path] is called Secret-of-All-Spiritual-Activities Intellect. It is called so because the influx that permeates itself is from the highest Blessing and the Supreme Glory." – Aryeh Kaplan translation.

What is the Secret?

"This is the secret of life: Man lives in God, and God lives in man. This answers all questions." – Egyptian *Bronzebook*, Book of Scrolls, 16:7.

That is to say, *all activities are spiritual and emanate from the One Source*.

The Number 8

Eight is a numeral symbol of rhythmic vibration. The curves are reciprocal and alternating. It is an endless activity. The two curves represent the paths of involution and evolution, the descending curve for involution and ascending curve for evolution. Eight symbolizes that all opposites are effects of a single cause and that balanced, reciprocal action and reaction between opposites results in harmony.

♌ - Leo

I Create – I am Special

Leo is a Fixed Fire sign. Being ruled by the Sun, Leo brings warmth, light, and life into the lives of their friends. Leo is self-confident, courageous, kind, generous, loyal, protective, honest and entertaining. These qualities negatively expressed becomes arrogant, greedy, sloppy, coldhearted, jealous, aggressive and vain.

Leo Attributes

Element: Fire. Identity. Inspirational. Intuitive. Spirit and Will. Activity. Excitable.

Quality: Fixed. Security. Stability. Persevering. Concentrative magnetic power.

Finds security and stability for identity through inspirational and creative activities. The search for secure and stable identity. Creative potential. Naive and fun-loving. Improvising its generosity to an appreciative audience. The sustained warmth of loyalty and radiant vitalization. Motivated by social insecurity. Flamboyant. Romantic. Authoritative. Self-expressive.

+   Vital outpouring. Giving. Creative. Impressively powerful. Charismatic. Loving. Enthusiastic. Dramatic. Affectionate. Honorable. Courageous. Self-confident.

-   Showy. Arrogant. Selfish. Dictatorial. Prideful. Protective of vanity.

Sun Rules Leo

Expresses self with warmly radiant vitality. Creative energy is colored by a sense of drama. Motivated by a need to be recognized for one's generosity. Radiates confidence and encouragement to others.

Saturn is in Detriment in Leo

Loyal and disciplined affection. The desire for security is fulfilled through achievements that express individuality.

Seeks to establish and preserve self through creative activity and self-expression. Fear and lack of trust in one's innate value and goodness can hinder self-expression and self-confidence. Pride and the urge for recognition are factors in accepting duties and responsibilities. Creative handling of responsibilities can produce deep happiness.

CHAPTER 10

Key 9 – The Hermit – Virgo

A snake belongs to the animal kingdom. The letter Yod (י) on Key 9 represents the hand of man. Thus, the power symbolized as a lion in Key 8 is shown on a wide plain, with a mountain peak in the background. But the Hermit in Key 9 stands at the summit of that same peak. He is male, in contrast to the woman of Key 8. The scene also contrasts the sunlit landscape of Key 8, for the Hermit stands holding a lantern to light the way for travelers toiling up the path toward the height.

Though his outward appearance differs, we find the Hermit on a mountain, like the Fool. The Fool fixes his gaze on a height ahead of him. So, likewise, the Hermit looks down as if surveying a path leading upward from the depths whence he has climbed.

Solitude, but not loneliness, is pictured by this Key. Superiority, because the Hermit is on a high peak, and his beard, that of the Emperor, symbolizes experience. So does the number 9 because it is the last of the series of numerals. Thus 9 symbolizes completion, and completion, applied to human life, is the attainment of adeptship and mastery. Those and many related ideas are represented by Key 9, which is the Tarot symbol of the perfected state of human consciousness.

That perfected state, however, is union with the One-Self. It is the state of absolute identification with the Master Power, which is meant whenever the Scriptures speak of the "Hand of God." All adepts and masters are, in very truth, God's hands. So are we, but we are far from being steadily aware of this great truth. We are like the hands of little children, full of potentiality but wanting practical skill. We have the powers, but we are deficient in training.

Yet even in our relative inefficiency, we are God's hands. Every work, whether done in wisdom or ignorance, is a direct transformation of power descending from the One Self. This is what the rays of the Hermit's lantern signify. Every man and woman on this planet is connected with the One-Self by a ray of cosmic light. We live and move by this One Power. All personal action responds to impulses coming down to us from this "Father of Lights."

Thus the supreme consciousness is the realization that the One Self is also the only Self. Thus Key 9 represents the completion of human attainment and shows an older man standing alone.

The zodiacal sign attributed to Yod is Virgo's sixth sign, and the lantern's six-pointed star is an allusion to the number of the sign in the zodiacal series. Virgo governs the intestinal tract, especially the small intestine, in medical astrology. In ancient pictorial representations, Virgo was shown as a woman holding a distaff (a spindle onto which wool or flax is wound for spinning). This was an allusion that the human body is woven from threads spun in the small intestine. Our food is changed into the basic substance from which the blood is charged with all the materials needed to function and repair our bodies.

The heights of adeptship are reached due to minute alterations in the chemistry and structure of the human physical body. Outwardly, an adept looks like any other member of the human race. But their blood is different. Their organs function better, and the rudimentary structures in most human skulls are fully functioning organs in the brain of a fully liberated master of life. The place where the fundamental difference between an adept's body and that of an ordinary man is determined is in the region governed by Virgo.

Virgo is ruled by Mercury, and in Tarot, Mercury is the Magician. This means that intelligent control of the body-building process changes the blood chemistry and the functioning of the physical organs. The making of such changes depends on the following:

1. Conscious knowledge of the use of self-consciousness for the right selection of food; and

2. Using the law pictured in Key 8 transfers the pattern of a higher and finer type of physical organism to subconsciousness.

The most important lesson in 9 is summed up in the word "response." It is the lesson we must learn that no act of human personality is self-originated. Instead, all acts of personality are truly Self-originated because they have their source in the One-Self.

Just as the Hermit, looking down, sees those climbing toward him, so the One Self Enters into the Lives of us all. To ourselves, we seem to be struggling upward, and only a few of us seem to be aware of any light from above. Still, the One-Self knows all its personal manifestations and works through everyone to bring about that person's conscious union with the Supreme Reality.

No human being is a puppet. Because all our personal activity is rooted in the freedom of the One Life, this freedom enters all we are or do. We misinterpret and misunderstand it, but we are right in our intuitive belief in free will. This duality in all human action does not mean responding to something outside or other than ourselves. It is a personal reaction to our true, innermost nature.

At his peak, the Hermit stands at the center of a great circle. His horizon is wider than that of any traveler below him. Many paths lead from all sides of the mountain to where he stands. The paths on one side are different from those on the opposite side and seem to go in opposite directions. Yet they all meet in one place. So do the various paths of human attainment differ in detail and in seeming direction. No two are precisely the same. Yet all lead to the same goal. That Goal is conscious identification with the one and only Self. This goal we are all destined to reach. The power which is expressed in the life of every human being is the power of that One-Self, and this power can never fail to perfect every detail of its work.

There may be lost souls if " lost " means "losing one's way." But sooner or later, the light of the Hermit's lantern will be a beacon to bring the wanderers back to the Path. And the better we understand Ageless Wisdom, the more it becomes evident that even the wanderers are never out of contact with the Eternal Light-bearer.

Symbols

The Hermit represents the consciousness of the individual who has attained enlightenment. He stands upon the mountain peaks as a light bearer for those below him on the path.

The Hermit's grey robe symbolizes the neutralization of the pairs of opposites because opposite colors mixed equally produce grey. The staff corresponds to Will and the Archetypal World. He stands in darkness because the Supreme Reality is dark and incomprehensible to our intellects.

The Hermit carries the golden six-rayed light, symbolizing cosmic principles and laws.

Practical Instruction

Use Key 9 to remind you that your true Self is, even now, all that your personal mind hopes and longs to be. Use it to deepen your understanding of the truth that there is never a moment when you are not under the watchful supervision of that same great "I AM."

Use this Key to convey to your subconsciousness the profound practical lesson of building a finer body. At this point in your study, you would most likely be confused by an elaborate explanation of the process. However, your subconsciousness understands every detail of the meaning of this Tarot Key and will respond to it by beginning to build the finer body you require.

Follow the same procedure as with the others. Be sure not to spend more than five minutes at a time on any Key. Remember, each is a portrait of yourself as you really are. Not what you want to be. WHAT YOU ARE. When you press out into actual manifestations of personal thought and speech and action as you really are, you will make evident to all the world that you are skilled in the fine art of Self-expression Tarot was devised to teach.

Yod – י

A Tongue of Flame or Hand

The letter Yod (י) is the fundamental Hebrew Letter. It is a tongue of Flame. From this letter, all other letters are formed. The letter name Yod (יוד) means "hand." This represents the hand of man, which creates on the physical plane and thus completes the work begun in the Higher Planes.

The upper point of Yod represents the Primal Will (Kether), while the rest of the letter corresponds to Chokmah (Wisdom). This implies that all mental activity is derived directly from the essential Will of the One Identity. This mental activity, or volition, takes form as the wisdom which is the basis for the entire cosmic order.

The Number 9

Nine is the number of the Foundation [Yesod, 9th Sephiroth]. It is a link between the higher worlds and Malkuth, the physical world. It also symbolizes completion, ending a sequence from zero (0) to nine (9).

Virgo – ♍

I Analyze – I Discriminate

Element: Earth. Material. Practical. Sense oriented. Pragmatic. Stable. Manifesting. Reliable.

Quality: Mutable Learning and Teaching. Changeable. Adaptive. Interactive.

Service and Health. Learning and teaching about the material and practical world. Selective processing. Prudent and judicious. Rearranging, refining and perfecting itself to remain useful and in service. Spontaneous (mutable sign). Helpful, humble and a need to serve. Discriminating-sorting the useful from the non-useful. Drive for improvement towards perfection. Discrimination is based upon critical analysis of the outcome of the action. Adjustment and judgment of self and life. Self-criticism. Detail oriented. Studious.

+   Dependable. Efficient. Modest. Humble. Willing to allow others in the limelight. Willing to admit when wrong. Organized. Thorough.

-   Critical of others and self (notice flaws). Skeptical. Prudish. Fastidious. Worrisome. Nervous quality. Picky. Matter of fact.

Mercury is Exalted and Rules Virgo

Communicates logically, critically, helpfully, humbly-sometimes negatively and skeptically. A need to discriminate among ideas and put them in a logical sequence to learn. Practical, helpful ideas contribute to the ability to make connections with others. Over-attention to details can hinder the perception of the larger viewpoint and all its interconnections and broader implications.

Jupiter is in Detriment in Virgo

Jupiter is the wise ruler that oversees his kingdom. Mercury in Virgo is good with the details. However, in Virgo's over-attention to specific details, Jupiter can inhibit his understanding of the big picture.

Seeks to grow and improve oneself through spontaneous helpfulness, dutiful service, and a disciplined approach to self-development. Humbly stays open to grace from a higher power and trusts the value of regular work and self-discipline. Over-attention to detail can inhibit connection with a larger order but usually has a well-developed critical faculty without excessive pettiness.

Venus is in Fall in Virgo

Venus is the goddess of love, art, and beauty. In the domain of Mercury, Venus sees the flaws in all works of art.

Expresses affection matter-of-factly, modestly, helpfully, timidly. A need to serve and be useful yields emotional satisfaction. Finds pleasure in precise attention to detail and analytical mental activity. A need for logic and practicality to feel comfortable and harmonious. Over-helpfulness, petty emotional criticisms or one's natural reserve can interfere with emotional give-and-take and the expression of passion.

CHAPTER 11

Key 10 – The Wheel of Fortune – Jupiter

Rotation is the keyword assigned to the Wheel of Fortune. Key 10 refers to the initial whirling motion in the vast expanse of the root substance of the universe. This is the Limitless Light. Differentiations of this primary motion cause all changes in form or quality on every plane.

The 8-spoked wheel is a symbol of this law and the force behind it. It manifests as the principle of rotation and evolution. It works through the entire series of cosmic manifestations as an intelligible principle. We can understand and apply it. It has been symbolized from time immemorial by a turning wheel.

The pair of opposites, Wealth and Folly, correspond to the meaning of Kaph. If our grasp of the meaning of events is weak, our control of things is uncertain, and our want of understanding manifests as poverty. On the other hand, a powerful grasp of the successive situations in our day-to-day experience brings wealth.

This wealth may be in dollars, or it may take other forms. Naturally, the money measure has its limitations, but it is safe to say that those who comprehend the situation of humanity in this world will never suffer material want.

Scientific comprehension takes facts like the recurrence of the seasons, the regularity of astronomical phenomena, and similar repetitive activities in the environment. Science observes and records. Then it makes deductions. Various systems are devised that record and predict cycles. This is what is behind the symbolism of Key 10.

At the outer corners of the picture are the Cherubic emblems (Bull, Lion, Eagle, and Man) mentioned in Ezekiel and Revelation. They represent the four fixed signs of the zodiac. The wheel itself is the symbol of the whole cycle of cosmic expression.

Sign	Element	Modality
Taurus, the Bull	Earth	
Leo, the Lion	Fire	Fixed
Scorpio, the Eagle	Water	
Aquarius, the Man	Air	

Thus the animals correspond to the four implements on the Magician's table, which stand for Fire (wand), Water (cup), Air (sword) and Earth (coin or pentacle).

Occult tradition associates these 4 elements with the Divine Name, Jehovah, written in Hebrew letters around the outer circle of the wheel. In English, these are represented by IHVH, and the total of their Hebrew (יהוה) values is 26. This is also the sum of the positions of Taurus, Leo, Scorpio, and Aquarius in the zodiac, these being, respectively, the 2nd, 5th, 8th and 11th signs (2 + 5 + 8 + 11 = 26).

Hebrew	Yod	Heh	Vav	Heh
	י	ה	ו	ה
Value	10	5	6	5
Element	Fire	Water	Air	Earth
Sign	Leo	Scorpio	Aquarius	Taurus

Alternating with the four Hebrew letters of IHVH (יהוה), the outer circle contains the Roman characters spelling the word ROTA, meaning – a wheel. From these four letters, the artificial word TAROT is formed by beginning at the top of the wheel and reading the letters clockwise around it, beginning and ending with T. From different arrangements of the same letters may be formed the rather barbarous Latin sentence, Rota Taro Orat Tora Ator, or, "The Wheel of Tarot speaks the Law of Ator."

Ator, an ancient Latin rendering of the name of the Egyptian goddess Hathor, personifying nature and corresponding more or less to Venus, is pictured as Key 3, the Empress.

All we can comprehend consists of activities that belong to the subconscious field of the Life-power's manifestation. "Nature" is just a generalization from our experiences, including the ancient classification of the four elements. What is at work in these fields is the operation of subconscious powers. This is why we can control whatever we can comprehend.

Within the outer circle showing the four Hebrew and the four Latin letters is an eight-armed cross. Four arms point to the Hebrew, and four to the Latin letters. The arms of the cross, pointing to the Latin letters, bear four symbols.

These are derived from alchemy. Beneath the letter T is the alchemical symbol of Mercury (☿). Near the letter A is the alchemical symbol for Sulfur. The symbol opposite the letter O stands for Salt. The symbol above the letter R is the sign Aquarius (♒), represented in the upper left-hand corner of Key 10 by a man's head. It is also the alchemical symbol for dissolution and the essential secret of the Great Work.

English	Hebrew Equivalent	Symbol	
T	Tav (ת)	Mercury	☿
A	Aleph (א)	Sulfur	🜍
R	Resh (ר)	Aquarius	♒
O	Ayin (ע)	Salt	⊖

Outside the wheel, a yellow serpent descends. It represents the vibrating force associated with the letter Teth (ט) and Key 8, involving itself in the conditions of name and form constituting our environment. The undulations in its body suggest vibration, representing the involution of the cosmic radiant energy, or Fohat, into the matter.

On the other side ascends a figure having a human body and a jackal's head. This is the Egyptian god Hermanubis, the soul's guide in its journey through the underworld, and closely related to Mercury and the Magician. It represents the evolution of consciousness from lower forms to higher.

His eye is opposite to the letter A, which is the Roman equivalent of Aleph (א). The intellectual consciousness of the advanced human being sees, more or less clearly, what is pictured in Tarot by the Fool (Aleph).

Few persons know the indwelling Spirit as a direct personal experience. Yet some have an intuitive perception of this Spirit, and thus the ears of Hermanubis are above the letter A. Though the intellectual consciousness may not experience super-consciousness directly, it can receive hints concerning that higher order of knowing through the channel of interior hearing or intuition as symbolized by the ears of Hermanubis.

The Sphinx is a synthesis of male and female, human and animal. The Sphinx is the real Self, having finished its evolutionary journey in this cycle of manifestation. It sits on top of the wheel. Under this creature is T, corresponding to Tav (ת), Key 21, and Administrative Intelligence. Thus the Sphinx, by its relation to this letter and to the Mercury symbol under the T, represents the completion of the Great Work.

To finish the Great Work is to develop the metaphysical senses. It is to directly express identity with the One-Self, and we must always remember that this experience is not to be confused with theoretical knowledge, philosophical speculation, or religious creed. The average human being does not even know about this identity. He believes or disbelieves without knowing the Self directly.

The exceptional human being does know, and because he knows, he shares consciously in administering the laws of nature. Therefore, his activities are always in harmony with how things are. He is adjusted to the cosmic rhythms. Thus whatever he does works out as planned, and he is free from the ups and downs of fluctuating fortune.

Practical Instruction

Use Key 10 to give you a better grasp of every situation which seems to be a problem.

Activities attributed to Jupiter and Key 10 require a certain level of faith, trust, and confidence in life and in ourselves. When your confidence is low, use Key 10 to realize that every problem and adversity will yield to the universal solvent or alchemical Mercury.

Humanity can observe the various appearances constituting its environment because of its self-consciousness. As a result, we discover their real versus their apparent nature. Thus we can reduce every form to its primal substance; whenever we do so, we find that substance to be the limitless Life-power symbolized in Tarot by the Fool.

Then, by exercising our power of mental vision in creative imagination, we can fix this primal substance into new shapes and forms. We may do this through indirect invention, using machines constructed by scientific comprehension. Or we may work only mentally upon the primal substance and bring forth forms corresponding to our images. They who can do this constitute the inner circle of adepts.

Kaph – כ

A Grasping Hand

Kaph is a grasping hand or the palm of the hand. To grasp is to take possession. To grasp anything with the mind is to become thoroughly familiar with it. What we comprehend is ours to control and use.

The Number 10

The summation of the numbers from 1 to 4 is 10. In Math, the notation is:

$$\Sigma 4 = 10$$

$$0 + 1 + 2 + 3 + 4 = 10$$

The stylized "E" (Σ) is called sigma.

Using Tarot Math, this means:

The power of spirit (Key 0) makes us curious and inquiring. If we observe (Key 1), remember (Key 2), imagine hidden relations (Key 3), and reason logically (Key 4), we shall comprehend (Key 10). Thus the Wheel of Fortune represents the full development of the meaning of the Emperor since 10 is the extension of 4.

The Planet Jupiter

૨|

Jupiter symbolizes the process leading to an expansion of consciousness, but at times, this expansion may be through ordeals and hardships. Jupiter is the planet of fortune, not a luxury.

Jupiter is attributed to the law, scientific research, philosophy, and religion. All these are human activities where we seek to expand our horizons. However, expanding our consciousness and obtaining a larger frame of reference without social interaction is impossible.

All these activities attributed to Jupiter require faith, trust, and confidence in life and ourselves. The study of religion and philosophy without faith is merely an intellectual exercise. The practice of law without trust and confidence in the ideals it represents leads to suspicion and cynicism.

Jupiter Summary

The principle of expansion, opportunity, success, prosperity, and growth. That which completes us and makes us whole. The urge to participate in the social realm. Grace. What draws you out and gives you optimism. Social laws. Cooperation. Civilization. How you seek to grow and trust in life. Consciousness expansion. Point of view and perspective. One's beliefs. Opportunistic aptitudes. What is amplified by faith. Intuition. Morality and code of ethics. Risks. Deals and gambles.

+   Faith. Reliance on a higher power or greater plan. Openness to grace. Optimism. Openness to self's need for improvement.

-   Over-confidence. Laziness. Scattering energy. Leaving the work to others. Irresponsibility. Over-extending self or promising too much.

Jupiter's Essential Dignities

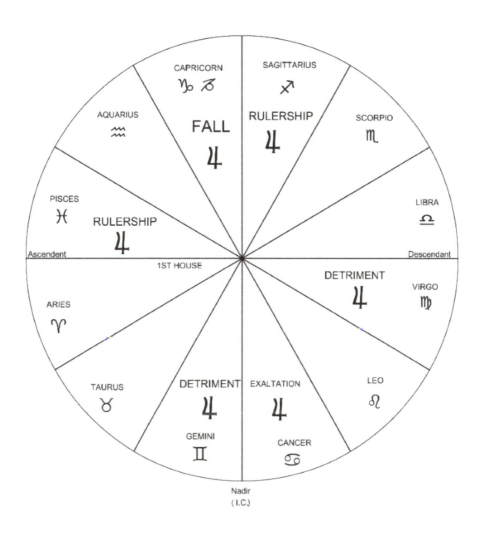

Jupiter Rules Sagittarius

Jupiter in Sagittarius is confident, optimistic and has an innate faith in life. In Sagittarius, Jupiter is dignified by Rulership and Triplicity by Night. Normally, planets in Sagittarius can suffer from foot-in-mouth disease. They say things "off the top of their heads" and, therefore, can hurt other people's feelings. By Night, Jupiter is introspective and thinks before he speaks. And is rewarded with a larger circle of friends.

Too much optimism can lead to over-extension of energy and overlooking the immediate possibilities.

Jupiter is in Detriment in Gemini

Jupiter is good at looking at the big picture but not so good with the details. In Gemini, Jupiter can be overwhelmed with too much information. As a result, optimism is sometimes hindered by excessive thinking and worrying.

Mercury-ruled signs naturally limit the expansiveness of Jupiter and thus make it harder for Jupiter to express himself. This is not without benefit. A manager is crucial to every artist. Sometimes we need someone to tell us what is and isn't possible.

Jupiter Rules Pisces

The Key phrase that describes Pisces is, *I believe*. Jupiter in Pisces is kind, caring and idealistic. Natives make good listeners. Jupiter attracts good luck when he is giving and compassionate. Helping others brings fulfillment.

Self-improvement can be hindered by unfocused, noncritical attitudes and escapism.

Jupiter is in Detriment in Virgo

Jupiter in Virgo is a humble scholar that believes his worth must be demonstrated through practical results – *dutiful*. Jupiter in Virgo has a strong sense of responsibility and expects too much from others – *perfectionists*.

Jupiter Is Exalted in Cancer

Cancer rules the home and family relationships. Jupiter rules the principle of social conduct based on mutual goodwill. Jupiter in Cancer can expand the concept of family to include a larger social whole. They can be emotionally sympathetic to people around them and treat them as family members.

Jupiter is in Fall in Capricorn

Capricorn is ruled by Saturn, the planet of discipline. Therefore Jupiter in Capricorn grows and improves oneself through hard work, discipline, and steady progress. They need to express qualities of self-control and confident conservatism to improve themselves. Optimism and expansion can be suppressed by an overly serious and fearful attitude. One's faith and trust are based on reality, experience, and an innate understanding of the value of history and tradition. Opportunities come through one's ability to be reliable, responsible, and patient.

CHAPTER 12

Key 11 – Justice

Lamed – ל

The Ox-goad or Shepard's Staff

Lamed (ל), the Hebrew equivalent of English L. Lamed, is a pictogram for an ox-goad or shepherd's staff. An ox goad is used to guide oxen and to keep them on the road chosen by the driver. Hence ideas of control and direction are connected with this letter.

Spelled in full, Lamed (למד) pronounced Lah.mad means to learn and study. Thus Lamed is related to ideas related to education.

The idea of education implied by Lamed is managing the pair of oxen, the super-consciousness typified by the Fool, and the intuitive knowledge symbolized by the Hierophant. To be educated is not to possess an accumulation of facts gathered from without. It is to be able to apply to the conduct of life the inspiration which comes to us from above (Fool) and from within (Hierophant).

Lamed is the second of three Hebrew letters formed like a serpent. Its shape is like that of a snake, uncoiled. The head is at the left side of the letter, the body is represented by the horizontal line, and the tail is indicated by the line dropping from the horizontal line at the right side of the letter. It symbolizes the serpent-power, coiled and quiescent in the Hebrew character for Teth (ט), extended and active.

The *Book of Formation* (*Sepher Yetzirah*) assigns action, or work, to Lamed. The individual who is truly educated is more than a possessor of information. This is a person possessed of practical skill. Education draws forth powers and develops the ability to apply them to the management and direction of affairs.

Observation and memory are the fundamentals of education. However, practical skill is the result of training which establishes habits, which are not fully established until our bodies, by the operation of subconsciousness, have been changed.

For example, a pianist's body and brain differ from those of one who cannot play. A pianist's hands have a characteristic shape, easily recognized. Whatever skill you may have has left perceptible traces on the structure of your physical mechanism. Thus we have said before that the difference between an adept and an average human being is a difference in physiology. An adept has practical knowledge and continually uses everything he knows.

Practical knowledge enables one to make adjustments. Hence the name of Key 11 is Justice. Abstract justice is law, and while it is true that human laws are often poor approximations of justice, the intent of laws is to establish a community governed in harmony with one another.

Venus Rules Libra. In Key 11, she is shown wearing a crown and seated upon a throne. Like the Empress, she represents creative imagination. All good work must be planned, and planning requires using the subconscious power to form clear mental images of intended actions.

Two things are necessary to make adjustments that change a problem into an achievement. First, we must weigh and measure the facts correctly. Without accurate measurements and correct standards, we are sure to fail. When we are content with guesses and approximations, we blunder along. Like oxen without drivers, our hit-and-miss procedure keeps us continually in difficulties.

Yet the facts are not enough. There must be action in harmony with our knowledge of the actual situation. Moreover, this action must be aimed at eliminating whatever restricts our freedom. Hence the scales of Justice are balanced by her sword, a symbol of terror to evil-doers.

Metaphorically, an evil-doer is any activity that restricts freedom and interferes with the harmonious adjustment of our lives. Therefore, whatever leads away from the path of liberation must be eliminated. You will notice that this detail of Key 11 is also a feature of Key 10, where the sphinx holds a sword. Remember, also, that Zain (ז), the sword, is the letter symbolized by the Lovers, a picture of two persons standing side by side like the two 1's in the number 11.

Practical skill in adjusting one's life is an application of the power of discrimination pictured in Key 6. Since 11 is the sum of 5 and 6, we may also say that practical skill is discrimination (Key 6) combined with intuition (Key 5). Unsurprisingly, we find many sudden flashes of intuitive perception among workers in scientific research. Such persons patiently seek facts, and their quest for truth requires them to develop great technical skills in manipulating delicate instruments.

Key 11 is the complement of Key 10, just as Key 1 is the complement of Key 0. The Wheel of Fortune is the Tarot symbol of cosmic law. Justice is the symbol of the application of that law through human action. Hence the central figure of Key 11 is a seated woman. Her position is passive and receptive, representing the subconscious side of our lives.

It may seem paradoxical to speak of passivity in connection with action. However, what is meant is that successful action is the mental state of agreement with the nature of things as they really are. Thus Key 11 is also connected with the idea of faith.

Faith, "the substance of things hoped for, and the evidence of things unseen," is the basis of right action. True faith is the habitual (therefore subconscious) conviction that nothing, whatever in the cosmic order, is hostile to man. On the contrary, whatever is, is for our good. When we have the wit to discover what is behind the appearances surrounding us, and the skill and courage to do what we know, we find that nothing in the universe is against us. Appearances to the contrary are due to our ignorance. When we measure facts correctly, especially about human nature, we can establish justice in our lives and surroundings.

Symbols

This Key is the center of the Tarot. It stands for equilibrium and balance, symbolized by the title, Justice, and the scales. This Key also symbolizes Karma, which literally means *Action* or *Work*. It manifests itself as the Law of Undeviating Justice. This is the Christian doctrine, *as a man sows, so shall he reap*. In physics, *every action has an equal and opposite reaction*. This is cause and effect.

The two curtains, suggesting duality, represent balance through their symmetrical arrangement. The circle and square on the front of the crown refer to the movement of Spirit within material forms. Finally, the sword represents discrimination, which is closely allied with the idea of Justice.

Key 11 is the agency through which all of the **forces** *represented by Keys 1 to 10 are transferred to the* **manifesting powers** *represented by Keys 12 to 21.*

This cryptic statement deserves a great deal of thought on your part. You will be well rewarded for your effort.

Practical Instruction

Use Key 11 to bring your daily activities into harmonious relations with others. It also serves to awaken a deep faith. Use it whenever you find it hard to get along with people. Finally, use it to bring you greater effectiveness in doing whatever is involved in your vocation.

The Number 11

"The general number of magick, or energy tending to change." – *777*, Crowley, 1977, p. xxv.]

"…11 is considered by Cabalists to be a number of evil signification in that it indicates by its very form a lie, that is, two Monades. This clear impossibility can only result from an illusion based on reflection." – *The Arabic Parts in Astrology*, Robert Zoller.

The number 11 is a pair of 1's. What is shown in Tarot by Key 1 and the Magician is unfolded, augmented, and extended by doubling. Since doubling is represented by the number 2 and the High Priestess, the Tarot meaning of 11 has to do with the recording and development accomplished by the activities represented by the High Priestess, and the result is balance. – Paul Foster Case.

Libra – I Relate

♎

Element: Air = Social. Intellectual. Conceptual. Thoughtful. Curious. Interactive.

Quality: Cardinal = Action. Initiative. Dynamic. Outgoing radiant force.

Equalizing tendencies. Adaptive and graceful. Harmonizing relations to encourage affinity and a sense of balance. Drive for completion through relationship. Initiates action on social and intellectual levels.

\+ Diplomatic. Socially appropriate. Refined. Beauty. Peaceful. Fair. Strong principals. Searching for balance. Aesthetic.

\- Superficial. Impractical. Phony. Vain. Flirtatious. Predictable. The imposition of principles and tyranny of ideals.

Venus Rules Libra

Venus is the goddess of love and personal relationships. In Libra, she is considerate, charming and socially correct. Venus in Libra has an eye for art and fashion.

Venus has a deep need for peace and harmony to feel comfort, but this could lead to avoidance of unpleasant emotional interchanges and thus limit intimacy.

Saturn is Exalted in Libra

Saturn is discipline, rules, and regulations. Saturn in Libra makes good lawyers, judges, mathematicians, and engineers since they understand relationships on human and scientific levels. Saturn in Libra is good at organization and public relations because they know how to do the right thing at the right time.

Saturn in Libra artist gives form and beauty through proper balance and proportion.

Fear (Saturn) of committed partnership (Libra) can hinder achievement and prevent a sense of satisfying intimacy. Therefore, a disciplined effort is put into maintaining relationships. Commitments, promises, and duties are honored and can bring deep satisfaction.

Mars is in its Detriment in Libra

Mars is action. In Libra, initiative and drive can be hindered by indecisiveness while one weighs options. Physical energy and decisiveness are strongly affected by one's close relationships and artistic influences.

The Sun is in its Fall in Libra

The Sun symbolizes your individuality and sense of self. In Libra, the sense of individuality is realized through relating with others. However, individuality can be compromised through over-concern about pleasing others.

CHAPTER 13

Key 12 – The Hanged Man – Neptune

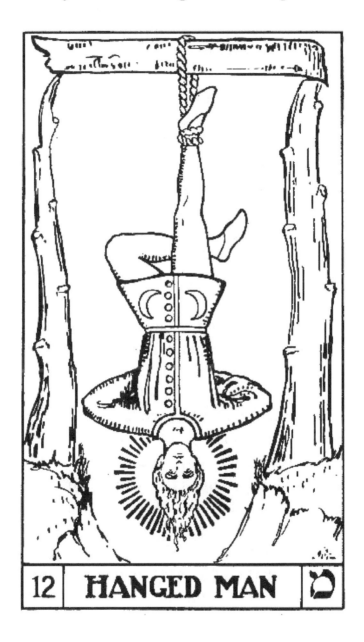

This picture symbolizes the adept's realization that his existence depends on Cosmic Law.

The Law of Reversal is frequently mentioned in Ageless Wisdom and is represented by innumerable symbols. Key 12 is the most important emblem in Tarot. Applying this Law of Reversal is one of the great secrets of occultism. The essential meaning of the law may be stated as follows:

To reverse the conditions of misery, disease, and failure and substitute for them their opposites of health, happiness, and success, it is necessary to think, speak and act in ways that are the reverse of those in which most persons think, speak and act. (That is, if what you're doing is not working, then try something else.)

One ancient statement of the Law of Reversal is given at the beginning of the Dhammapada, an important summary of Buddha's doctrine:

"All that we are is the result of what we have thought. It is founded on our thoughts. It is made up of our thoughts. Therefore, if a man speaks or acts with an evil thought, pain follows him as the wheel follows the foot of the ox that draws the carriage.

"All that we are is the result of what we have thought: it is founded on our thoughts. It is made up of our thoughts. Therefore, if a man speaks or acts with pure thought, happiness follows him like a shadow that never leaves him.

"Hatred does not cease by hatred at any time: hatred ceases by love. This is an old rule."

Yet it is not enough to say, "If you want to be happy and successful, you must learn to reverse your thinking." Instead, we require a practical method that will affect the necessary reversal.

The proper use of Key 12 is such a method. Looking at this picture will do wonders in reversing our ordinary habits of thought and speech. However, to get the full suggestive power into operation, it is useful to know the correspondences and meaning of Key 12. This understanding forms a bridge that easily carries the suggestions into our subconsciousness.

The letter Mem (מ) printed on this Key is the equivalent of English M. Mem means water.

Water reflects everything upside down. It reverses the images cast upon it. The occult water is not the fluid we draw from kitchen taps. One alchemical writer says: "The ignorant, when they hear us name water, think it is the water of the clouds; but, if they understood our books, they would know it to be a permanent or fixed water." Another writes, "Our water is a heavenly water, which wets not the hand." And a third, "Water is the mother, seed, and root of all minerals."

Alchemical Water spreads over a vast expanse, like a great sea. It moves in waves. It flows in currents and forms itself into whirlpools or vortices. It also takes form in drops or corpuscles.

In short, occult water is the Astral Fluid, the electromagnetic energy which is the substance of all things. It is called the seed of minerals because every mineral comprises atoms, and every atom contains "drops" of this primary substance.

This apparently abstract idea has immediate use. Many practical marvels of recent inventions have been made possible by developing the conception of the electrical constitution of matter.

But what difference does this make to an ordinary human being?

One thing which makes mental and occult practice difficult is the supposition that what we have to do demands the exertion of an intangible mental power against the inertia of a tangible physical reality. This "matter" surrounding us is so dense, resistant, and hard to move that most people cannot believe that mere thinking has any power over it.

A practical occultist is not deceived by surface appearances. He knows that material things have neither the solidity nor the inertia which his unaided senses report. He understands that the densest physical substance and the lightest gases are formed from tiny, widely separated "drops" of the cosmic Water.

Thus, we approach a problem by changing our thinking. Practical occultists know there is no essential difference between the energy which takes form as thought and that which takes form as a diamond or a piece of metal.

By reversing our mental attitude toward the conditions of our environment, we free our minds from that subjection to appearances. With thought power, we can change our conditions for the better.

Key 12 shows a Suspended Man. This suspension is achieved by concentration and leads to the release of amazing powers, which give an adept perfect control over his mind, body, and environmental conditions.

The individual who has this experience reverses his attitude toward life. They habitually think and feel themselves to be a vehicle for the manifestation of the limitless power of the cosmic Life-Breath. Gone forever is the delusion that personality is separate from the total universal activity.

When Jesus said, "Of myself, I can do nothing," he expressed this realization. The words are no confession of weakness. On the contrary, they tell the truth that even the least of personal actions is a particular manifestation of universal laws and forces. Instead of lessening the importance of personality, this realization adds to that importance. It shows that the real value of personality is found in the fact that a person is an agency whereby the limitless powers of the One Life may be brought to bear in controlling the conditions of this field of relative existence.

This Key symbolizes the real world, hidden from the ignorant by their delusions. They who succeed in reversing their conception of personality realize that the real world is, so to say, the body of God. They know they are a member of that body. They know nothing anywhere in the real world that is inimical to humanity or opposed to their welfare. On the contrary, they depend utterly on the real world's adequate support.

The gallows are in the form Tav (ת). Its 12 lopped branches are the 12 signs of the zodiac. Tav corresponds to Key 21, The World. Tav represents the power of limitation called Saturn and the element Earth. To be suspended from the letter Tav, therefore, means this:

To reverse the conditions of negative experiences which trouble us, we must know that all human use of the Life-power depends on the principle of specialization. This is the limitation of the Life-power to some particular form of expression.

We use this principle when we concentrate. It is what is meant by the Magician's pointing finger. It is what makes our mental imagery so potent. To succeed, this imagery must include mental pictures of specific actions and definite results expressed in conditions on the physical plane. The Emerald Tablet tells us that One Life's power is integrating if it is turned into Earth.

Hence the Magician has a coin as one of the tools on his table. His work is not finished until he understands and applies the principle of values on the physical plane.

Like the Hermit and the Emperor, the Hanged Man's hair is white. But his face is youthful. Thus, he combines the Life-power, Eternal Youth and the Ancient of Days.

The glory around the Hanged Hangman's head symbolizes the illumination from the suspending activity of personal consciousness. This Glory is the same as the sun in Keys 0 and 6.

The white rope which suspends the Hanged Man in the middle of the cross-bar indicates that concentration is the basic principle of this practice.

The rope itself is white, representing the universal light energy. It comprises many strands, twisted into spirals because the cosmic life force takes spiral forms in all its manifestations.

The feet of the Hanged Man is shod in yellow. Yellow is the color of Key 1. This is a punning allusion that true understanding of our personal situation is arrived at by actively exercising our intellectual powers.

Thus the legs of the Hanged Man are dressed in red, forming a figure which refers to Key 4, the Emperor. Red typifies the active use of power. A trance is an intense state of concentration and mental activity. The mind of one in the state of Samadhi is still, just as a spinning top is still, because it is moving rapidly in an unbroken flow of knowledge revolving around a single point of consciousness.

The Hanged Man represents a pendulum at rest. He is unmoved and immovable because he realizes that no person ever thinks, moves or acts of himself but expresses the thought, motion, and action of the ONE IDENTITY.

The Hanged Man's jacket is blue and refers to the element of Water. It is trimmed in silver and has two lunar crescents, ten silver buttons, and a silver cross. All these refer to the powers of subconsciousness, which means:

One arrives at the reversal of usual personality interpretations by practicing mental exercises, including acts of reflection and recollection. The secrets of life are not on the surface of things. One must be still to know. In stillness, one begins to be able to read the scroll of the High Priestess. And one of the truths is the ten basic intelligible aspects of the Life-power's activity – "ten, and not nine, ten, and not eleven," as we read in The Book of Formation. One also learns that the cross's true meaning has to do with an increase since the cross is the original form of the letter Tav. This sign is still used as a symbol of addition and multiplication.

The arms and head of the Hanged Man establish the points of a triangle. His legs suggest the number 4.

Thus this whole figure represents a combination of 4 and 3, but with the 4 reversed, it occupies the superior position.

In Tarot, Key 4 is the Emperor, and 3 is the Empress. To put 4 over 3 is to make reason the dominant element and to subordinate imagination to logic. Yet one must remember that the 4 is reversed. The logic of the average human being, who bases his reasoning on superficial appearances, is opposite to that of an adept who knows inner realities.

The average human being is dominated by false images. Their reasoning is nothing but rationalization. The more they "reason," the worse the situation. They are victims of delusion.

Adepts have learned what mental images shall occupy their attention. Therefore, they select images with care. This enables them to imagine creatively and reach a true vision of humanity's place in the cosmic order. Adepts succeed in controlling their world because they understand the real meaning of their personality.

Practical Instruction

Use Key 12 as a focus for concentration. You will discover far more for yourself than written here. You will begin to weave the strands of consciousness, eventually establishing an understanding Key 12 symbolizes.

When the pictorial suggestions take effect, they will initiate changes in your mind and body. As a consequence of these changes, you will adopt the mental attitude of utter dependence on the One-life. From this mental attitude, health and well-being follow automatically. Key 12 serves to correct the negative states of mind. Thus it eradicates the causes of failure because the essence of human personality is identical to the Limitless Life, which creates and sustains the universe.

The Number 12

The number 12 is composed of two digits, 1 and 2. Therefore, twelve expresses the idea of the manifestation of 2 through the activity of 1. Hence the Tarot meaning of 12 is the outpouring of the powers of subconsciousness (Key 2) through the fixation of self-consciousness in acts of attention (Key 1).

This is precisely what the Hanged Man typifies. When concentration is prolonged, the direct experience of the super-conscious state of being results. This is the perfect union of the personal with the universal consciousness. It is attained by practices that quiet the mind and suspend the formation of chains of ideas.

Mem – מ

Mother Letter of Water

Mem is one of the 3 mother letters. It is assigned to the element of Water. Mem is numerically forty (40). This is the number of days and nights it rained during the Biblical Flood and the weeks of the gestation of a human child. It is the number of years the Israelites wandered in the desert. Thus, it symbolizes hidden growth and development before a new birth or beginning.

"At that time, the universe was made, and then Earth received her form. It slept warmly amid the waters, which were not the waters of Earth, and this was before the beginning of life and earthly substance, I am the God of Creation." – *Egyptian Bronze Book, Gleanings*, 15:41.

The Planet Neptune

♆

Principle: Transcendent freedom. Unification. Freedom from ego-self.

+ Expression: Attunement with the whole. Realization of the spiritual dimension of experience. All-encompassing compassion. Living an ideal.

- Expression: Self-destructive escapism. Evasion of responsibilities and self's deepest needs. Refusal to face one's motives and to commit self to anything.

The principle of unification and transcendence; urges us to return to harmony and unity. Service and self-sacrifice. Escapism. Neptune is a higher octave of Venus. Venus-personal love, Neptune-universal or unconditional love. Our highest ideals and expectations. Disillusionment. Dreamtime. Mysticism. Where we disappear.

Modern Rulership

Uranus, Neptune, and Pluto are planets discovered with the invention of telescopes. The authors disagree on Neptune's signs of Exaltation, Fall and Detriment. However, astrologers do agree that Neptune is the co-ruler of Pisces.

The best way to understand Neptune is to observe people with Neptune in Pisces. However, Neptune entered Pisces in 2011 and will leave in 2026. Therefore, the oldest people with Neptune in Pisces were 7 years old in 2018. It will take decades before these individuals grow up so astrologers can observe the effects of Neptune in Pisces in their charts.

CHAPTER 14

Key 13 – Death – Scorpio

The card represents *change*, *motion*, and *transformation*. Death is but the gateway to a larger life in reality. The power symbolized by Key 13 transforms our consciousness and releases it from the limitations that hinder its free expression. Life is continual motion, change, and disintegration for the release of energy.

One main contrast distinguishes Ageless Wisdom from ordinary human philosophies. At their best, the speculations of ordinary human reason on the questions of survival and immortality give us no more than hopes based on analogy. At their worst, they lead to the hopeless conviction that this world and its conditions are all we can know. Ageless Wisdom offers us a practical method for annulling death. This is a method based on human experience. Human beings like ourselves have practiced it successfully in times past. Men and women living now have triumphed over death.

For such persons, the grave has no terrors, death no sting of loss or separation. Theirs is no hope. It is a certainty, and they say we may share their knowledge.

To practice this method, we don't invite doubts about our sanity by declaring, "There is no death." On the contrary, we must face resolutely the ever-present fact that bodies die. Denial of this fact is folly. We never understand anything we try to deny.

Airplanes were not invented by denying that objects heavier than air fall to the ground. Everything in a plane is heavier than air. We admit all the facts, and then we recognize, in certain combinations of other facts, a means to overcome the force of gravity.

We face an undeniable fact when we come into the presence of death. But, equally undeniable is the fact we can overcome death by calling into operation other laws and forces, which are always at hand, ready for our use.

Part of every human being is immortal, something not born with the body but will never die. But, more than this, the immortal something within us brings about the dissolution of our physical bodies.

Our essential immortal nature is the cause of our physical death. When we face death and learn its meaning, we shall discover how to overcome it.

This is more than a promise to survive the body's death. It is more than a hope of resurrection. It is more than a change of consciousness. The knowledge of those who are consciously immortal totally annuls death. Those who become perfect in this knowledge here on earth need no experience of physical dissolution. They are released from what seems to be the "common lot." They can maintain the existence of their physical bodies in perfect health and vigor, limited only by their own deliberate choice.

Key 13 symbolically declares this doctrine of Ageless Wisdom. It conveys to subconsciousness, through the sense of sight, stimuli that will call forth from our inner mind the knowledge which will enable us to annul death.

At first glance, the central figure of Key 13 is the conventional representation of the "Grim Reaper." However, the skeleton reminds us that the body's bony structure is the foundation of all our muscular activities, growth and development.

This something is the One-power, specialized in the body's reproductive functions. It is the Seed-power. Hence a conventionalized picture of a seed is placed in the upper left-hand corner of Key 13.

The two ovals are united, or really one. The inner and smaller oval represents the source of radiant energy. From it proceed five rays, representing the five differentiations known as Ether, Fire, Water, Air, and Earth. This radiant energy fills the space enclosed by the outer oval with the inner oval. The INNER POWER projects itself, or what appears to be an extension of itself, as SPACE (the larger oval) and fills that space with forms of energy whose combination constitutes the body of the universe.

The same power is represented by the skeleton. All growth and development are based on endless permutations of form. In the absolute sense, there is no change. The No-Thing remains eternally Itself throughout the whole series of appearances. Yet, in the relative sense, this transformation is actual and necessitates the dissolution of useless and outworn forms.

Look closely, and you will see that the skeleton is curiously distorted. There are two twists in the spinal column. One is just above the pelvis and marks the location of the Mars center. The other is at the neck near Venus. Were this skeleton clothed with flesh, its body would be twisted in a way no contortionist could duplicate. This anatomical impossibility indicates the central secret of Key 13.

We have to learn to give a certain twist to the energy manifested through the Mars center. This is the center that controls the reproductive activities of the body. We must turn this energy in another direction, the reverse of what it usually takes.

The Mars force is present in the body during one's entire lifetime. Therefore, we cannot annul death unless it is deliberately TURNED in the right direction.

This new direction is given to the Mars force utilizing the activity of its complement, the Venus center in the throat. This is affected by a change in mental imagery; thus, we have another bit of light on the meaning of 13 here.

The right way to effect the necessary minute changes in our chemical and physiological makeup is to imagine new life patterns. Make the right patterns, and subconsciousness will handle the corresponding physical alterations. The new image must precede the new structure.

In Key 13, the direction of movement is from North to South. The skeleton walks toward the right side of the picture. The wind blows the branches of the trees in the same direction. In occultism, the north is the side of the dark, disintegrative forces assigned to Mars. South has to do with regenerative activities and the Sun. What is pictured in Key 13 is the movement of a current of force from the Mars center, just below the navel, upward toward the Sun center, above and behind the heart.

The movement of a current of nerve force from the Mars center passes through the solar plexus (Jupiter center) to the Sun center. This rising energy current is set moving in response to certain activities of the Venus center in the throat. This results in new specializations of the force which enters the physical organism through the Sun center, such as electricity entering the wiring system of a building through the main switch. Hence this Key shows a rising sun in the background to intimate the beginning of a new cycle of manifestation for those powers symbolized by the Sun.

The energy of this rising current of nerve force continues after it leaves the heart center. It sets in motion special functions of the higher centers in the throat and head (the Venus, Moon, and Mercury centers or chakras). This results in a change of consciousness, accompanied by the manifestation of occult powers latent in most human personalities.

Among these is the power of remembering the experiences in the astral body and other higher vehicles. All persons "travel" more or less in these higher vehicles when the body is asleep. We say "more or less" because such "journeys" are not nightly occurrences. We put the words "travel" and "journeys" in quotation marks because there are good reasons for believing that what seems, during such experiences, movement from place to place is actually simply an extension of consciousness.

Just as soon as one begins to have a conscious waking recollection of such experiences, you are freed from the delusion that personality depends on having a physical body.

The higher powers developed after this initial awakening are represented in Key 13 by the hands and feet, which the skeleton reaps. His scythe has a handle shaped like the letter "T" to show that this occult work calls into play the power coiled in the Saturn center at the base of the spine.

The skeleton scythe is made of steel, the metal of Mars. It is crescent-shaped, indicating a relation between this and Key 2. The three hands, two active and one passive, represent works. The severed foot refers to the end of the Piscean age, as the rising sun begins the Aquarian age. The man's head in the bottom right-hand corner symbolizes Wisdom (Chokmah), and the woman's, Understanding (Binah). The white rose is the same as that carried by the Fool in Key 0. In some astrology schools, this represents Uranus's exaltation in Scorpio.

Practical Instruction

This Key is intended to help you imagine yourself as free from the bondage of physical and temporal existence. It will aid in setting in motion the subtle inner activities which propel the force from the Mars center to move up instead down. It will do what is needed in this direction without any weird concentration exercises intended to arouse the activity of body centers.

Study this lesson until you grasp the real import of death. Then picture yourself as being what you are, free from bondage to the physical body. Eventually, you will begin to receive the confirmations we have outlined briefly in this lesson.

Nun – נ

The letter Nun (נ) printed on this Key means, as a verb, to sprout, to grow. As a noun (נון), it means *fish*.

In the human body, this power of growth develops a structure through the multiplication of cells. It is also the fundamental principle of reproduction. Therefore, the letter Nun is associated with Scorpio, which presides over reproduction. Also, Scorpio is assigned to the eighth house of the horoscope, the house of death and inheritances.

OUR MOST PRECIOUS HERITAGE IS THE POWER THAT MANIFESTS ITSELF IN THE FACT OF DEATH.

The nature of this power is indicated by the number 13. In Hebrew gematria, this is the number of Achad (אחד), meaning *unity*. The other means love, beloved, אהבה. The *One-power* where all things proceed, the *Love-Power*, which is the cause of all attractions and affinities, is also the *Death-power* which brings about the dissolution of physical bodies. There are not two antagonistic powers, one making for life and the other for death. There is only *One-power* having opposite forms of manifestation.

Scorpio – I Desire

♏

Element: Water. Feelings. Emotional. Soul. Psychic. Empathic.

Quality: Fixed. Security, Stability, Persevering. Internal.

A search for emotional and soul security. Penetration through intense emotional power. Search for truth. Confrontational. Intense and resourceful. Catalyzing change to provoke greater emotional honesty and growth. See things as black and white. Sex. Will. Life and death issues. Magic and occultism. Regeneration.

+   Great integrity. Intensity. Passionate. Sexual. Persevering. Secretive. Depth. Transformation. The ability to undergo great change. Healing self and others. Deeply spiritual and truthful. Wants to penetrate the surface to find out what things are made of.

-   Extreme. Vengeful. Suspicious. Domineering. Controlling. Jealous.

Mars Dignities

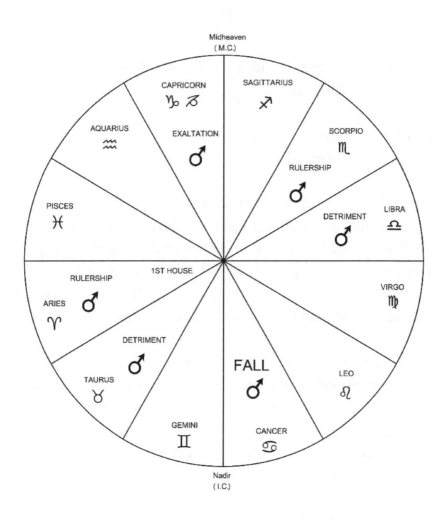

Mars Rules Scorpio

Asserts self intensely, magnetically, passionately, and powerfully. Strong desires, compulsions, and challenges prompt physical energy and initiative. Capable of great endurance. Sex urge is motivated by the need to share a deep emotional closeness and to experience profound intensity. Need to channel and transform emotional power to achieve desires effectively. Decisiveness and freedom of expression are hindered by secretiveness and the need for self-protection and control.

Venus is in Detriment in Scorpio

Venus is the goddess of love, and in Scorpio, she seeks to possess the object of her desire. However, people are not possessions. Expresses affection intensely, obsessively, with consuming feelings. The urge for pleasure is colored by compulsive desires, depth, and passionate emotions. Needs can be hindered by an inclination to secrecy and trust issues. Needs to penetrate deeply into a relationship with intense emotional power to feel close to another.

The Moon is in its Fall in Scorpio

In a fixed Water sign, the Moon seeks emotional security and stability by trying to possess the object of their desire. However, loved ones are not possessions; this nurturing style doesn't work well.

Uranus is Exalted in Scorpio

Uranus is Key 0, The Fool, the immortal part of you. The Lord of Life is exalted in the sign of Death. Because in the sign of Scorpio, Uranus has overcome death.

CHAPTER 15

Key 14 – Temperance – Sagittarius

Verification is the basic meaning of Key 14. This picture represents the process whereby we prove the accuracy of the principles and laws laid down in Ageless Wisdom. It shows us how we may confirm our beliefs and theories. It indicates how we may establish the truth of what we are taught.

Verification is made through testing and trial that every aspirant must pass before reaching the heights of Initiation. The Initiate must balance all their vehicles. An initiate no longer goes to extremes but has mastered the pairs of opposites by choosing a middle path between two extreme courses of action.

Truth is established by trial. To know, we must do. Fluency in using the language of Ageless Wisdom is no guarantee that we are competent to perform the Great Work. We must subject our theories to the laboratory tests of everyday experience.

Temperance is used in its archaic meaning, the act of tempering or mingling, modification, or combination. Therefore Temperance means regulation and the measured proportion of constituent parts.

The Great Work combines and harmonizes the various elements which enter into the constitution of human personality, blending them together in one whole.

By the solar disc and the Sun and rays behind him, we know the central figure is the archangel, Michael. He is the angel of the Sun and the element Fire. Michael also corresponds to the angel described in the tenth chapter of Revelation.

"Then I saw another mighty angel descend from heaven. He was clothed in a cloud, and a rainbow encircled his head. His face was like the sun, his legs were like pillars of fire, and he had a little scroll open in his hand. He set his right foot on the sea and his left foot on the land, and he uttered a great shout like a lion's roar;

Notice the connection between the solar angel and the seven thunders, which uttered things the seer was forbidden to write. The thunderbolt is the special emblem of Jupiter (♃), ruled by Sagittarius (♐), to which Key 14 corresponds. Sagittarius is the Archer, and the Hebrew name for this, Sagittarius (קשת), is also the name for the rainbow.

One significant difference exists between the angel in Revelation and Key 14. The angle in Key 14 has a vase and a torch instead of a scroll. Yet the meaning is the same. The little scroll is the scroll of the Law, which the High Priestess holds. When that scroll is unrolled, the Law is made manifest or put into operation. In Key 14, the operation of the Law is shown by what the angel does.

The Divine Name, Jehovah (יהוה), written on his breast, identifies the angel with the One-Reality. Commonly we think of angels as being different from the One-Life, of which they are messengers. But, in truth, they are aspects of that One Life. That which was, is, and is to come to IHVH (יהוה) is the Reality that presents itself to us under all guises.

The 7-pointed star under the Great Name refers to the 7 Spirits of the Life-power. These are 7 great phases of the One Conscious Energy – the 7 Spirits of God. The 7-pointed star also represents the works of man because the 7-sided figure cannot be drawn geometrically but requires measuring tools.

The vase, from which water is poured, represents the cosmic reservoir of conscious energy. We all make contact with this through subconsciousness. The waterfalls in a triple stream indicate that we make contact with this power through subconsciousness. However, the combined super-conscious, self-conscious and subconscious activities are necessary for performing the Great Work.

The stream of water falls on a lion, a symbol of Leo (♌), to indicate the modification of animal nature by the powers of human consciousness. Here is a suggestion for blending contrasting elements, Water and Fire, and their equilibrium.

The torch in the angel's left hand represents the consumption of physical forms by the fiery action of the Life-power. From it falls five flames, each shaped like a Yod (י). They refer to the fivefold differentiation of the Life-Breath into Ether, Fire, Water, Air, and Earth.

These flames fall on an eagle, a symbol of Scorpio (♏). They symbolize what is shown in Key 13 by the seed symbol with its five rays proceeding from the inner oval. This conveys the idea of blending opposites and the resulting equilibrium because the eagle symbolizes Water and Scorpio. The eagle, moreover, is the bird of Jupiter (♃), the ruling planet of Sagittarius (♐). Notice in the sky map that the Eagle Constellation is above Sagittarius.

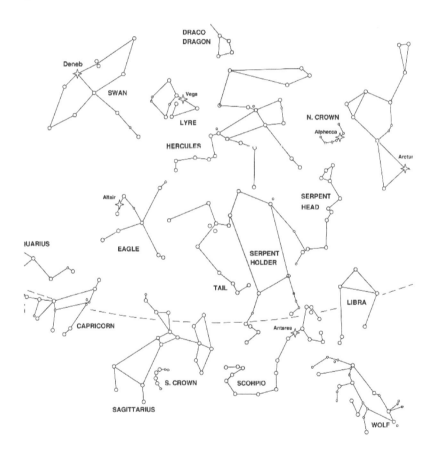

The end of the path in Key 14 is a crown suspended in the air. It represents the first of the ten Qabalistic

Sephiroth, *Kether*, and the Crown. It symbolizes the culmination of the Great Work, which is the perfect self-knowledge indicated by the statement, "The Father and I are ONE." The twin mountain peaks are Sephiroth, Wisdom (*Chokmah*) and Understanding (*Binah*).

The pool represents consciousness, and the physical earth is formed. The angel stands on both to show that the Great Work is a psycho-chemical operation wherein transformations of mental states bring about corresponding changes in the bodily organism.

Practical Instruction

The central idea of Key 14 is that we can verify Ageless Wisdom's teaching through personal activities. In so doing, we change our bodies so the brain can perceive the Primal Will expressed through our lives.

By using it as a focus of concentrated attention, we can keep the real meaning of daily experience steadily in mind. Then we will come to know that occult doctrine is true.

The practice of the mental states evoked by Key 14 is the *practice of the presence of God* or the *Knowledge and Conversation of the Holy Guardian Angel*.

Samek – ס

Samekh is the third of the three serpentine letters in the series (Teth ט and Lamed ל). It represents a snake with its tail in its mouth, thus symbolizing completion and eternity.

As a verb, the letter-name Samekh (סמך) means *to prop, bear up, uphold, sustain, and establish*.

This letter is similar to the final Mem (ם). It is a modification of the circle and symbolizes a serpent swallowing its own tail. Note the serpent girdle on Key 1, The Magician.

The Number 14

Fourteen (14) is the numeral value of זהב, *zawhab*, gold. This is the gold of enlightenment, the philosophical gold that represents perfect and verified truth.

Sagittarius – I Perceive

♐

Element: Fire. Identity. Inspirational. Intuitive. Spirit and Will. Activity. Inspired. Excitable.

Quality: Mutable. Learning and Teaching. Changeable. Adaptive. Interactive.

Philosophy. Religion. Inspiration. Idealism. Academic matters and sports. Spacious. Seeks sufficient consciousness expansion to confirm its views and opinions. Restless aspiration propels one towards an ideal. Willing to believe in new ideas. A desire to know.

+ Idealistic. Spontaneous. Frank. Extroverted. Restless. Exploration. Adventurous. Expansive. Generous. Cheerful. Optimistic. Seekers. Blessed with the luck that comes from their attitude.

- Hypocritical. Exaggerators. Careless. Gypsy-like. Indulgent. Blunt. Looks at the big picture without consideration of the details. Opinionated.

Jupiter Rules Sagittarius

Jupiter in Sagittarius is confident, optimistic and has an innate faith in life. In Sagittarius, Jupiter is dignified by *Rulership* and *Triplicity* by Night. Normally, planets in Sagittarius can suffer from foot-in-mouth disease. They say things "off the top of their heads" and, therefore, can hurt other people's feelings. By Night, Jupiter is introspective and thinks before he speaks. And is rewarded with a larger circle of friends.

Too much optimism can lead to over-extension of energy and overlooking the immediate possibilities.

Mercury is in its Detriment in Sagittarius

Mercury in Sagittarius has a thirst for knowledge and little patience for dry facts of academics. In Sagittarius, Mercury is optimistic. However, the same optimism can blind them to reality.

CHAPTER 16

Key 15 – The Devil – Capricorn

The principle of contrast running through the Tarot is obvious in comparing Keys 14 and 15. The angel of Temperance is an angel of light. Key 15 shows an angel of darkness.

Key 15 is one of the most important Tarot Keys. It is a symbolic veil for the greatest practical secret of occultism. It both conceals and reveals the secret of the powers ascribed by tradition to Moses, David, and Solomon. This is the same secret Pythagoras learned in Egyptian temple schools. It is the Great Arcanum of alchemy and magic. To know it is to be able to make the Philosophers' Stone and the Elixir of Life.

Yet those who know it cannot tell. The essential point is beyond the power of words to express. If you already know it, you can decide whether this lesson's writer also knows it. If you are ready to learn it, this lesson will plant a seed in your mind, eventually growing into knowledge.

This knowledge is interiorly received and perceived. Then, finally, the meaning dawns on us. When this occurs, there is no doubt, guesswork, or uncertainty. One knows and knows that he knows.

The first clue is that the letter-name Ayin (עין) means *eye*, *fountain*, and *outward appearance*. Key 15 is a picture of the way things look rather than a picture of the way they really are. And yet we must remember that every Tarot Key is a picture of humanity. Tarot symbolizes some aspect of the One-Self manifest in the innumerable personalities that constitute the human race.

The word Devil is from a Greek noun which means slanderer. Key 15 stands for everything, or anything, which gives a bad opinion of the worth and value of our own real nature.

The Devil represents the delusion of outward appearance. Key 15 is the opposite of Key 6. Key 15 shows what happens when we fail to use our faculty of discrimination.

Key 15 represents the One-Power as it appears to those who take its appearances at face value. When we look at the world surrounding us, we see a composite of incongruous elements mixed in what seems to be hopeless confusion. Of this confusion, the impossible mixture of male and female, human and animal, which is the central figure of Key 15, is an example. Nothing like it exists, yet everything in it is some aspect of reality. Yet, suppose we understand these appearances, their origins and their purpose in the cosmic order. In that case, we shall understand Eliphas Levi's cryptic saying, "The Devil is God, as he is misunderstood by the wicked."

The Bible says the serpent was created on a day when the Lord looked at all He had made and pronounced it "very good." God created the universe with His own substance. Therefore the appearances which deceive us and are the causes of our fears and our poor opinion of human nature have no other source than the One-Power, which is always working for our good.

Capricorn, assigned to the letter Ayin has a connection with the Devil. For the ancient Egyptians called the adversary Apep or Apophis (Greek – Typhon). Apophis is the origin of much that is attributed to His Satanic Majesty.

Symbolic representations of Capricorn include:

1. A monster having the head and body of a goat and the tail of a fish;
2. A crocodile with the head of an elephant;
3. A donkey;
4. The mysterious monster is represented in Job and Revelation as Leviathan and the Old Serpent.

However, Capricorn is the sign which represents the birth of the Redeemer. Just after the Winter Solstice, which marks the beginning of Capricorn, the sun moves northward, and the days get longer.

Our Yule festival comes to us from the Druids and the cult of Mithra, whose birthday was December 25 (three days after the winter solstice). Capricorn is a feminine sign related to the mother power, which brings forth the Savior.

Ayin (ע) is assigned to the Renewing Intelligence. The Qabalistic commentary says that by Renewing Intelligence, God renews all that is begun afresh in the world's creation. Here is a hint in plain sight that the power that tempts and destroys is the same one that renews and saves.

Even in this supposedly enlightened age and free country, there are many places where it would be dangerous to make a plain statement about some things written in this lesson. It is dangerous for the teacher and some pupils because they would almost certainly pervert and misapply the teaching.

Eliphas Levi says: "Satan, as a superior personality and power, has no existence. The devil is the Great Magic Agent, employed for evil purposes by a perverse will." To this, we add that perversity will result from ignorance.

The inverted pentagram is a symbol of evil magic. It represents the inversions of the powers of normal humanity when man misunderstands himself and, in his thinking, inverts his true position. The outcome of his error is the hideous image of the Adversary.

The Devil is an androgyne, having one male and one female breast. From the pentagram to the extremity of his right-hand horn, there are 10 divisions, and on the other horn, there are 12. These represent the 22 forces corresponding to the letters of the Hebrew alphabet.

The Devil has the ears of an ass because the donkey is one of the symbols of Capricorn. His face is that of a goat, though it looks human. This part of the symbolism refers to the sexual manifestation of the Life-power, termed libido by psychology. Yet, as Geraldine Coster says, "When we define libido as instinctive energy, we ought to realize that we are speaking of what many Christians would call the Holy Spirit."

The Devil's gross, hairy body suggests the element of Earth. In colored versions of this Key, it is painted an earthen brown. Its massive proportions suggest the ponderous powers of the physical plane.

He has bat wings. They are wings of darkness because bats fly at night. They symbolize the occult agencies whereby the forces of the physical plane, and the powers of instinctive energy, are transported from place to place or transmuted from one form to another.

The eagle's legs and talons refer to the sign Scorpio, the element Water, and the letter Nun (נ).

The symbol of Mercury on the Devil's belly refers to the control exerted by the self-conscious mind over the force symbolized by the demon. The upper part of the Mercury symbol is yellow, and the cross is red. Thus the whole symbol represents a combination of powers of Mercury (yellow) and Mars (red) that is exalted in Capricorn.

On the uplifted right hand of the Devil is the astrological symbol for Saturn. This hand makes a gesture that says, "There is nothing hidden. What you see is all there is." This is the primary falsehood that leads to all manner of disastrous results.

The inverted torch in the Devil's left hand is similar to the torch in the angel's hand in Key 14. It burns smoky and gives little light. It is a symbol of the inverted use of the Mars force. The black background is a symbol of darkness and ignorance.

The two human figures are personifications of self-conscious and subconscious minds. Their horns and hoofs symbolize delusions that bestialize human consciousness. In addition, the figures are chained to a half-cube, a symbol of half-knowledge of the physical plane. This represents *Bondage*.

Earlier in this lesson, we said the Great Secret cannot be told. Thus what we say in conclusion must be developed by each of our readers as he progresses in understanding.

THERE IS NO DEVIL if one means an evil, malicious, independent principle or personality opposed to God. But, on the other hand, THERE IS A DEVIL if, by this term, you understand the divine power of materialization, which seems to enclose the Limitless Light within the boundaries of three-dimensional existence. This is the power that apparently subdivides the One-Life into many separate lives.

Yet this same power is what redeems, renews, enlightens, and finally liberates us. The Adversary is overcome when we understand what it really is and knows what we are. The name of the Adversary is *Legion* or *Multiplicity*. The consciousness which overcomes it is the realization of *Unity*.

Practical Instruction

How may this realization of unity be developed? By the exercise of the power called **Mercury**. By attention, by observation, by forming correct interpretations and right plans. Then the very power which holds us in chains becomes the force that sets us free. The opponent who sets the problems that now are puzzling us becomes the Master of the Game, who helps us to find the solutions and play with skill.

The Number 15

The Devil is YOU, just as truly as the Fool, or the High Priestess, or the Hierophant is you. The number 15 shows that despite his ridiculous and repulsive appearance, this Devil is a manifestation of the truth revealing the power of super-consciousness, symbolized by the Hierophant (Key 5), acting through the agency of the observing function of self-consciousness symbolized by Key 1.

Capricorn – I Utilize – I Make Use of

♑

Element: Earth. Material. Practical. Sense oriented. Pragmatic. Stable. Manifesting. Reliable.

Quality: Cardinal. Action. Initiative. Dynamic.

Initiates activity (cardinal) in the material, the practical world (earth). Status. Ambition. Politics. Law. Reliance on social structures. Self-organizing. Sober and dignified. Establishing integrity by attaining mastery. Impersonal determination to get things done.

+   Good at planning and organizing. Ambitious and seeming selfish, but when attaining goals, gives freely. Hard-working. Cautious. Responsible. Disciplined. Efficient. Paternal.

-   Fearful. Selfish. Insensitive. Pessimistic. Conservative. The ends justify the means.

Saturn Rules Capricorn

Seeks to establish and preserve self by attaining one's ambitions, authority, and societal position. Strongly disciplined efforts expended toward planning the fulfillment of one's responsibilities. Overly-developed organizing ability can lead to attempts to control all situations too tightly. Urge to defend integrity through determination, hard work, and cautious behavior. Excessive fear of disapproval can hinder the full achievement of one's aims. Deep-seated need to be reliable and depend on one's own resources.

Mars Is Exalted in Capricorn

Mars in Capricorn is a good organizer and works hard. In a cardinal Earth sign ruled by Saturn, Mars is self-disciplined and likes to be in control. This position brings admiration rather than love from the opposite sex.

People with Mars in Capricorn are practical and ambitious; they make good, efficient workers. Their desire to achieve importance and prove their powers drives them to work steadily to attain high standing in their careers and respect from the world.

Moon is in its Detriment

Saturn is disciplined. The moon is emotion. Moon in Capricorn is emotionally reserved but resourceful and enterprising. However, because of the Mars influence of Capricorn, the Moon can be easily irritated and become impatient.

CHAPTER 17

Key 16 – The Tower – Mars

Key 16 is attributed to the second stage of spiritual unfoldment, *Awakening*. It represents the flash of clear vision that reveals the true nature of our being, which has been hidden because of *bondage* (Key 15). The tower is the structure of error and ignorance. It is struck by the lightning of truth emanating from the central sun of Pure Being. The crown is willpower. It is the false crown of personal will. Right knowledge begins with a flash of comprehension.

True Will is symbolized by Key 9, The Hermit. What is over-thrown is the delusion that we exist as separate personalities. This is the cause of all human suffering and limitation.

The first stage of spiritual unfoldment is fear, ignorance, and misery. Ageless Wisdom understands this stage to be necessary. Unhappy as are those persons who have not advanced beyond it, they are by no means victims of blind laws which do not take human life into account. Nor are they forgotten children of an absentee Deity, too careless to provide for their welfare. Least of all, they suffer from malignant hindrances devised by a personal Devil. Their state is the necessary consequence of the nature of the creative process. Creation is by evolution and progressive development, from relative limitation and restriction to greater freedom. This process of man's progressive liberation is divided by Ageless Wisdom into seven stages, corresponding to the last seven Tarot Keys.

We can control ourselves and our circumstances by translating mental perception into words. Basically, we think in pictures. Hence Key 4, the Emperor, is associated with the sense of sight. Until we can say what we see, and until what we say agrees with things as they really are, we cannot plan our actions intelligently.

All control of thought is word control because every definite idea can be put into words. Desirable conditions are brought to pass by the right use of language. Conversely, sickness, misery, and failure follow the wrong use of words. Our house of life is built of words, and we must be wise in selecting and arranging.

Key 16 is full of symbols that relate to language. Once they are pointed out, they are obvious.

The tower is built from 22 courses of masonry. Twenty-two Yods hang in the air. Every Hebrew letter is developed from the letter Yod. Hence the 22 Yods are symbols of the powers represented by the Hebrew letters and the Tarot Keys.

They hang in the air because one principle of Ageless Wisdom is this:

*The forces of life that enter into thought also take form in all **physical things**. These forces have no physical basis. They are self-supporting and the foundation of everything else.*

Consequently, 10 Yods are on one side of the tower, forming the Tree of Life. This is the diagram of the 10 basic aspects of Life-power intelligible to humans. They also represent the 3 elements, Fire, Air, and Water. The fourth element, Earth, is the synthesis.

On the other side of the tower are 12 Yods, corresponding to the letters representing the 12 signs of the zodiac and the 12 basic types of human personality. These letters are grouped to suggest the outline of figure 8, with a dot in the center of each loop. In this connection, remember 8 is the value of Cheth (ח) corresponding to Speech and Key 7. Unfortunately, we cannot develop the meaning here. However, we bring it to your notice to show you how carefully the Tarot was designed.

The twenty-two courses of masonry in the tower symbolize the wrong use of words. They are built of the same basic matcrials, but the arrangement is wrong.

The tower is built of bricks, and so was the Tower of Babel, to which it alludes. "Bricks instead of stone" is one secret of the meaning of the Bible allegory. Wherever stone is employed in symbolism, it means conscious union with Reality. The reason is that eben, stone (אבן), is a combination of the words Ab (אב), father, and Ben (בן), son.

In Hebrew, brick (לבנה) is spelled the same as the noun meaning moon. To substitute brick for stone is to substitute what may well be called "moonshine" for the true consciousness of our identity with the Parent Source of all existence.

This moonshine is more poisonous than any product of the Tennessee stills. It is the false knowledge resulting from the race mind's memory of man's imperfect appraisal of himself and his circumstances.

Another name for it is common sense –what most people think and say. It is always in opposition to science. It is always the enemy of progress. It is the "rule of thumb" consciousness of those who take appearances at face value. It is expressed in popular proverbs and superstitions. If we try to live by it, we are in trouble.

No two people who believe in common sense will agree on what it really is. "Common sense ought to tell you," we hear people say. What do they mean? Usually, "If only you were the superior person I happen to be, you would agree with me."

To try building your house of life with the bricks of common sense is to be afflicted with the curse of Babel. There is no unity of opinion among persons whose interpretations of experience are based on looking at things instead of looking into them.

The fundamental error of common sense is that every human being is a separate entity, possessed of powers of his own. This is a philosophy of isolation. So the tower in Key 16 stands on a lonely peak.

Egypt and Rome were firmly convinced that their civilization would endure forever. Yet every great nation has fallen. The civilizations fall because they are based on common sense. All accepted the superstition of racial superiority. All were cruel and greedy. All believed the superior race had the right to enslave inferior peoples. All accepted and practiced economic and political theories, which set class above class. All ground the faces of the poor to enrich a small minority.

The lightning flash in Key 16 comes from a solar disk, indicating that the Life-power is an illumination source. This flash of true perception knocks off the crown of spurious superiority.

The crown also represents the false notion that there is any such thing as an independent personal (or national) will. The only free will in the universe is the Primal Will. The power of that Will flows through us but does not originate in the field of personality. We have the use of this free Will, just as we use radiant energy, which is its physical manifestation.

The lightning flash starts a fire that will ultimately destroy the tower. In the second stage of spiritual unfoldment comes a sudden flash of perception that upsets all our opinions and seems to destroy the foundations of our personal existence. But we shall see that the apparent catastrophe is succeeded by another stage of unfoldment.

Notice that the falling figures are fully clothed, in contrast to the nude figures of Key 6. One of the results of the sudden illumination is that both aspects of personal consciousness undergo a reversal of opinion. Self-consciousness and subconsciousness always disguise themselves from each other until awakening comes. They are always more or less at cross purposes.

Practical Instruction

Use Key 16 as a means to overcome your superstitions. Use it to free your mind from being enslaved by common sense.

Use it also whenever you are confronted by what seems to be a problem. For example, you have a problem because you are ignorant. You are ignorant because, hitherto, you have accepted some appearance at face value. You are in trouble because your words express faulty reasoning.

Key 16 will help you overcome this misuse of language. You need not believe it. Just try it. You will be delighted at the way your subconsciousness responds.

The Number 16

The number 16 is the power of 6 (The Lovers and discrimination) expressed using self-consciousness (Key 1, the Magician). The reduction of 16 is 7. Key 7, The Chariot, is directly connected with the idea of speech.

Peh - פ

Peh (פ) is the equivalent of English P. Peh is a mouth as an organ of speech. Compare Key 16 with Key 10. You will see that the character of Peh (פ) is the same as Kaph (כ), with something added which looks like a tongue in an open mouth. This is just what Peh stands for, the open mouth as the organ of speech. In Deuteronomy 8:3,

> So He humbled you, allowed you to hunger, and fed you with manna which you did not know nor did your fathers know, that He might make you know that humanity shall not live by bread alone; but humanity ha-adam (האדם) lives by every **word** that proceeds from the mouth of (פי) the Lord (יהוה).

The mouth is an organ of expression. Ayin (ע) on Key 15 is the eye as an organ of impression. Furthermore, Peh being a Kaph with a tongue, stands for the articulate expression of scientific comprehension, symbolized by The Wheel of Fortune.

Mars - ♂

How we assert ourselves. Sex drive. Penetration. How we go about getting what we want. Motivation. Muscular system. The will to act. Action. The Warrior archetype. Aggression. Willpower. Mating behavior. What we fight for.

+   Courage. Initiative. Willpower is consciously directed toward a legitimate aim.

-     Impatience. Willfulness. Violence. Improper use of force or threats.

Mars' Dignities

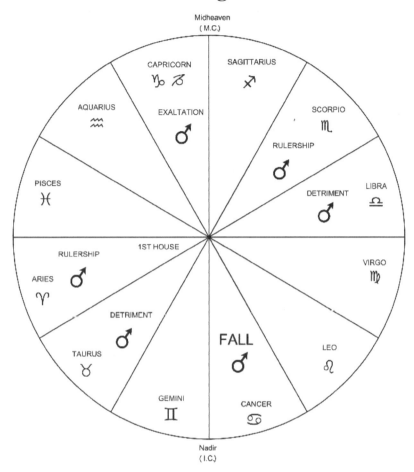

Mars Rules Aries

Asserts self competitively, dynamically, and impatiently. The single-pointed release of physical energy directed toward a new experience. A flair for starting new businesses and/or mechanical ingenuity. Faces obstacles directly, but recklessness can impede success. Sexual drive and physical energy are expressed impulsively, powerfully, and confidently.

Mars is in its Detriment in Libra

Mars asserts self sociably, cooperatively, charmingly, with direct relatedness. In Libra, Mars' initiative and drive can be hindered by indecisiveness while one weighs options. Physical energy and decisiveness are strongly affected by one's close relationships and by aesthetic influences.

Mars Rules Scorpio

Asserts self intensely, magnetically, passionately, and powerfully. Strong desires, compulsions, and challenges prompt physical energy and initiative. Capable of great endurance. Sex urge is motivated by the need to share a deep emotional closeness and intensity. Need to channel and transform emotional power to achieve desires effectively. Decisiveness and freedom of expression are hindered by secretiveness and the need for self-protection and control.

Mars in its Detriment in Taurus

Mars in Taurus asserts itself steadily, practically, retentively, conservatively, and stubbornly - often with a creative and/or artistic flair. Initiative and drive are colored by material concerns. Physical energy and sexual drive are influenced by an appreciation of the physical senses.

Venus rules Taurus, and this influence tends to make Mars lazy. However, a leisurely pace is not the same thing as idleness. Mars in Taurus is a slow starter but often goes farther than most. Mars in Taurus works best at a steady pace.

Persistence is their virtue. Physical efficiency and comfort are inseparable. Ordinarily, Taurus is good-natured. And though they are slow to anger, their rage is fearfully destructive when it is aroused.

Mars Is Exalted in Capricorn

Mars in Capricorn is a good organizer and works hard. In a cardinal Earth sign ruled by Saturn, Mars is self-disciplined and likes to be in control. Mars in Capricorn is practical and ambitious; it makes for good, efficient workers.

Mars is in its Fall in Cancer

Asserts self sensitively, shyly, indirectly, and sympathetically. Temperamental. A need to feel connected with one's roots and traditions to clarify one's desires and understand one's direction in life. Initiative and willpower can be hindered by moodiness and cautious self-protection. Capable of fearless action to support loved ones. Physical and sexual energy and decisiveness are inhibited by unconscious feelings, fears, and vulnerabilities and stimulated by feeling cared for and protected.

CHAPTER 18

Key 17 – The Star – Aquarius

The third stage of spiritual unfoldment is Revelation, symbolized by Key 17. With this Key, we come to the Tarot doctrine of meditation.

If it is true that none of us does anything of or by ourselves, it must be true that when we meditate, something is done through us rather than by us.

The Book of Tokens says,

"One of the profound doctrines is the universe owes its existence to the Creator's perpetual self-recognition. Nature is thus the result of the Spirit's meditation upon the powers of its own being. The universe is thought into existence and is maintained in existence by thought. Upon this foundation rests the whole structure of practical occultism. From this doctrine, you may understand the importance of meditation.

"Whenever aspirants meditate, they share in the exercise of the divine power that creates everything. Thus one of the tests whereby a student may know whether or not he has really succeeded in meditation is this: Let him find out whether or not what he has been doing takes form in the production of something better than he had before he began to meditate.

"The Divine Mother is always unveiled before her lord. In man, except in those rare moments when he participates in the Divine meditation, she is at best the veiled Isis, and at worst the demon of the fifteenth Key."

Key 17 is attributed to Aquarius. This is written (דלי), and its number, 44, is that of the noun Dam (דם), blood. Blood is the *Water-bearer* in the human body. The *blood* is the *Astral Fluid* of the occultists because all the elements entering into its composition are specialized forms of the radiant energy which comes to us from the stars.

This cosmic radiant energy is sent out from the various suns, or fixed stars, throughout the universe. In Key 17, these numerous energy sources are pictured as the single great star over the woman's head. This star also symbolizes what alchemists call the quintessence, the fifth or last and highest power in any natural body.

The star has 8-principal rays so that it is a geometrical correspondence to the eight spokes of the Wheel of Fortune. It also corresponds to the ten symbols of Spirit on the dress of the Fool.

The 7 lesser stars correspond to what the alchemists" call their metals. These are the same as the 7 chakras of the Yogis. They are also the interior stars of esoteric astrology. They are 8-pointed to indicate their correspondence to the great star.

The two stars on either side of the great star, distinguished from the others by their interior rays, are symbols of the Sun and Moon. The whole arrangement is as follows,

MARS   VENUS

SUN   MOON

MERCURY

SATURN   JUPITER

The tree represents the human organism and particularly the brain and nervous system. The bird on the tree is an ibis, a fishing bird whose beak has the same meaning as the letter Tzaddi (צ). Because the Egyptians associated the ibis with Thoth (Hermes), this bird corresponds to the Magician in the Tarot.

The woman is the same as the Empress (Key 3) and in Strength (Key 8). Note the reduction of 17 is 8, the number of Strength. This same woman will appear again as the World-dancer in the last Key of Tarot.

Aquarius is ruled by Saturn (co-ruler Uranus). Thus the main figure of Key 17 is the same Saturn pictured in Key 21 as a dancer. Yet this same figure is also the Empress or Venus. There is an occult sympathy between Saturn and Venus, which is indicated throughout the texts of Ageless Wisdom.

The woman also represents truth, and in meditation, the truth about Nature is shown to us without disguise. Hence the woman is nude.

The weight of her body rests on her left knee and is supported by Earth, representing the facts of physical existence. She maintains her balance with her right leg. Her right foot rests upon the waves on the surface of the pool, thus indicating balance attained by control of vibration. In meditation, something gives solidity and supporting power to the ordinarily unstable mind stuff symbolized by Water. Alchemists refer to meditation when they speak of the "fixation of the volatile."

The two vases stand for the two personal modes of consciousness, self-consciousness and subconsciousness. The ellipses on their sides symbolize the zero sign, which stands for Spirit, the No-Thing.

From the vase in the woman's right-hand falls a stream which sets up a wave motion in the pool. This represents the activity of subconsciousness brought about by meditation. A stream falls on land from the other vase and divides into five parts, representing the perfection of the five senses by practicing meditation.

The mountain is the same as Keys 6 and 0. It represents the perfection of the Great Work, which controls the inorganic forms of the Life-power's activity. In alchemy, this is termed the "mineral work." It is the final achievement of occult practice.

Notice the contrast between the scene of terror in Key 16 and the peaceful picture in Key 17. It symbolizes that Nature unveils herself to us in meditation after the storm and stress of awakening.

Unless we have been awakened by some crisis in our lives, we never enter into this third stage of unfoldment - Revelation. So long as we remain isolated in the fancied security of our tower of personal isolation, we are still in the dark.

Practical Instruction

Use this Key with Key 5 to draw from within the right answer to every problem. Remember that your problem is an indication of your ignorance. Bait the hook of meditation with an intense desire for light on your immediate problem. Be specific. Don't sit in silence with your mind open to anything that may happen to come.

A fisherman varies his bait according to what fish he wants to catch. If you use Key 17 to help you meditate, you will find that it aids you in getting light on every difficulty.

Tzaddi - צ

Tzaddi (צדי) means a man lying on his side. Spelled צדה, it means to *lie in wait, ambush, lurk,* and *scheme.* This symbolizes the means of investigating the unseen. That is research into the depths of inner consciousness, symbolized by water. Such hunting for inner knowledge is the function of meditation.

Aquarius – I Know

♒

Element: Air. Social. Intellectual. Conceptual. Thoughtful. Curious. Interactive.

Quality: Fixed. Security. Stability. Persevering. Internal. Concentrative magnetic power.

Detached focus. Inventive. The search for intellectual and social stability. An unpredictable style of interacting to sustain its social freedom. Detached coordination of people and concepts. Little sense of individual self. Often define themselves by the group they associate with. The tendency to think about others. Science. Music. Genius. Political movements and revolutions. Humanitarianism, group, and collective ideals.

+   Independent. Original. Fair. Inventive. True individuals. Innovative. Value their right to be their own person, not followers. Humanitarian.

-     Detached. Eccentric. Contrary. Rebellious. Reactionary. Rebel/Reformer. Uncomfortable with emotion. Impersonal.

Saturn Rules Aquarius

Seeks to establish and preserve self through disciplined mental abilities, clearly defined knowledge, and commitment to social or futuristic goals. Well-developed ability to organize groups of people and/or concepts. Works well in groups, often guiding this group's energy toward specific achievements, but needs to preserve independence. Urging toward eccentricity can jeopardize the chance for tangible achievement. Just and fair in dealing with others. However, some people may misinterpret it as cold and indifferent.

The Sun is in its Detriment in Aquarius

Sun in Aquarius is original, independent and freedom-loving. Strong likes and dislikes. Unpredictable, curious and intellectual. Creative energy is directed toward society as welfare and theoretical concepts, especially through innovation. Radiates friendliness and people-oriented mental energy-often with a tinge of extremism. The urge to be and to create is colored by freedom, eccentricity, and experimentation. Expression of individuality can be deterred by self-effacement, over-concentration on duty, or aimless rebellion.

CHAPTER 19

Key 18 – The Moon – Pisces

The fourth stage of spiritual unfoldment is *Organization*. This organization is carried out by the subconscious processes controlled from the back of the head. This part of the head contains the Occipital lobe, where the sight center is located. It also houses the cerebellum, which regulates coordination and muscular activity.

Qoph - ק

The letter-name Qoph (קוֹף) means the *eye* of a needle and the *hole* for an ax handle. Spelled קף, it means *circle* and *to go around*, specifically, the *circuit of the Sun*. **Not** the Sun, but the path the Sun takes. Note that Key 18 shows a path that starts from the pool of water and leads to the heights of adeptship.

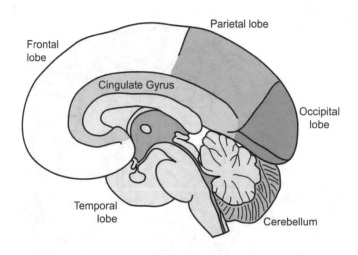

By NEUROtiker - Own work, CC BY-SA 3.0,
https://commons.wikimedia.org/w/index.php?curid=2653584

Below the cerebellum is the medulla oblongata.

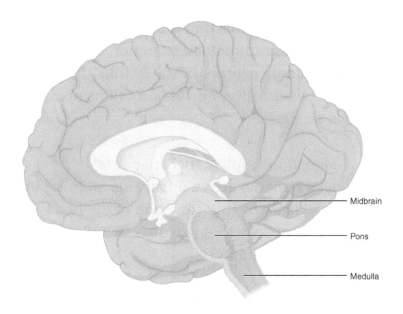

By OpenStax -
https://cnx.org/contents/FPtK1zmh@8.25:fEI3C8Ot@10/Preface,
CC BY 4.0,
https://commons.wikimedia.org/w/index.php?curid=30147954

The medulla oblongata regulates breathing, heart and blood vessel function, digestion, and swallowing. In addition, the medulla unites the brain with the spinal cord. Thus it is the connecting link between the higher centers of sensation, thought and action in the head and the subordinate centers in the trunk. This knot of nerve cells keeps us alive, and its functions are carried on while we sleep.

Sleep is assigned to Qoph (ק) because this consciousness remains active during sleep. In addition, occultists have learned that the back of the head contains groups of cells that are directly influenced by the practice of suggestion.

Treatments depending on affirmations are based on the law of suggestion, no matter what may be the theories held by persons who give such treatments. The fact that every metaphysical healer gets about the same percentage of healings as any other indicates this clearly.

The principle is always the same. Using words, or other devices, the healer helps the patient to form a specific image of the desired result. He makes his patient expect this result. Then the desired image is impressed on subconsciousness.

This image is transferred from the upper brain, through the Moon center behind the root of the nose, to the Venus center in the throat. From the Venus center, it radiates through the entire sympathetic nervous system. At the same time, it is transferred to the cells of the medulla and from them to the cerebrospinal nervous system.

Thus the Moon center (pituitary body) and the medulla may be considered two related centers. The pituitary gland is connected with the sympathetic nervous system, the medulla with the cerebrospinal system. They are both relay stations between the brain and the body. Impulses pass through them, downward from the brain and upward from cell groups in the trunk and limbs. There is a close connection between the Moon center (chakra), the High Priestess, and those of the medulla, represented by Key 18, the Moon.

Key 18 has to do with the physical body and its activities. This is important because much-pretended occultism assumes that the Great Work aims to separate human personality's "higher principles" from the physical body. Beginners are often led astray by these false doctrines. Those who do NOT know are forever talking about the "thralldom of matter." They create the impression that the body is an enemy, that there is something evil in flesh and blood. They teach that it is desired to suppress the physical organism and subdue its normal functions.

The truth is the exact opposite. While we live on the physical plane, our task is to refine our physical bodies, purify them, and effect subtle changes in their structure. A true occultist aims to begin where nature leaves off and go on to perfect the work of evolution, which nature cannot complete without man's cooperation. The Great Work aims to build a perfect physical vehicle, which shall be truly a "temple not made with hands, eternal in the heavens."

Do not be misled by that last word. We live in the heavens now. Jesus was very clear about the location of the Kingdom of Heaven/God.

> "Being asked by the Pharisees when the kingdom of God would come, he answered them, "The kingdom of God is not coming with signs to be observed, nor will they say, 'Look, here it is!' or 'There!' for behold, the kingdom of God is within you." – Luke 17:20-21

In Key 18, the Moon has 16 principal and 16 secondary rays, 32. These represent the 32 Paths of Wisdom represented by the Tree of Life. These powers are woven together to make the human personality and bodily vesture. Subconscious powers, symbolized by the Moon, are the active agencies in this operation.

Corporeal Intelligence, or Body Consciousness, is attributed to Qoph. The Hebrew word translated as "Corporeal" comes from a root that means "to rain upon," and the Yods (׳) in Key 18 is a reference to this. In the colored version, these letters are red and yellow, representing the life force fixed in the chemical composition of the blood. These falling Yods say in symbolic language: "The power of YOD is what descends into physical embodiment. It is the power of the Will of the Ancient of Days."

On either side of the path, battlemented towers form a gateway. The design suggests that each tower is connected to a wall. This is the wall that marks the limits of normal sensation and perception. Yet it is not a final boundary. Beyond it lies a vast region of experience, and the way leading into that region is open for all who dare to follow it.

The dog and the wolf are animals of the same canine genus. The wolf is the result of natural evolution. The dog is a product of human adaptation. Thus the dog represents art, in the widest sense of that term, while the wolf represents natural conditions that may be modified by artistic adaptation.

The path lies between these extremes of art and nature. In the foreground, it traverses a cultivated area, bounded in the middle distance by the towers representing human attainments. The field of experience is available to all humanity because it is within the limits of normal sensation.

The path leads beyond this into blue distances representing the planes of consciousness we may enter when we have changed our bodies, chemically and structurally. This region of the Beyond may also be entered during sleep and trance. Still, knowledge so gained is imperfect because it has to be brought into the field of conscious awareness through a physical body not yet adapted to the higher orders of knowing.

The rise and fall of the path refer to the law of periodicity. This idea is related to the various symbols of polarity represented by the High Priestess. Yet, though there are ups and downs along relatively short distances on this path, the road itself is a continual ascent. The path passes between these two extremes because the way of balance is neither too far towards artificiality nor too far towards ungoverned natural impulses.

It begins in a pool representing life activity's universal subconscious plane. This is the same pool we have seen in Keys 14 and 17. From it rises a crayfish, an animal wearing its skeleton outside and using that bony carapace as a shield against attack. It symbolizes the early stages of unfoldment, in which the student considers himself separate from the rest of nature.

The alchemical dictum, "First the stone, then the plant, then the animal, then the man, and finally the god," is suggested by the stones and plants at the edge of the pool, by the crayfish, dog, and wolf, and by the path and towers – the former marking the progress of man, and the latter, structures built by him. The path leads through the opening marked by the towers. The ground undulates, representing alternate periods of rest and action.

Pisces governs the feet, and a path worn by human feet is a conspicuous symbol in Key 18. Occultists often use puns to fix their doctrine in the minds of their pupils. Hence the feet are said to represent understanding.

This is why the sign Pisces is associated with the Way of Liberation and Body Consciousness. However, until we understand the principle involved, we cannot apply it. The principle is this:

All manifestation is light vibrations. On the physical plane, the expression of the higher powers requires the presence of suitable physical instruments. These instruments must be built within the human body by an extension of the process which has brought the body to its present stage of development.

Practical Instruction

Use Key 18 to evoke from your subconsciousness its deep knowledge of the truth that spiritual unfoldment here on earth necessitates physiological transformations. Practice with this Key sets in motion activities whereby subconsciousness applies its natural control of the body to effect minute alterations in blood chemistry and the structure of cell groups. Ultimately this makes the body a suitable instrument for performing Great Work.

The Number 18

Number 18 expresses the power of 8, manifest through the agency of 1. Key 8 is a symbol of control of animal nature, having special reference to the functions of a Sun center near the heart. Key 1 symbolizes the direction of subconscious powers using acts of attention. Key 8 represents the power of the *Sun*. Key 1 is *Mercury*. Key 18 is named "The Moon." By number and title, this illustration corresponds to the alchemical dictum:

> *The Great Work is nothing but the operation of the Sun and Moon, performed with the aid of Mercury.*

The alchemical process is a physical process directed and controlled by mental means. It aims at a transformation of the human body. When this transformation is effected, the adept has a physical vehicle by which he can exercise unusual powers, including the ability to transmute metals. His body is his laboratory, and its organs are the alchemist's "secret vessels."

Pisces – I Believe

♓

Element: Water. Feelings. Emotional. Soul. Psychic. Empathic.

Quality: Mutable. Learning and Teaching. Changeable. Adaptive. Interactive.

Absorbing. Vulnerable and imaginative. Impressionable. Mystical. Psychic. Dissolving boundaries to realize all-encompassing unity. Learning and teaching through experience with feelings. Healing compassion for all that suffers. Pisces lives in the feeling world more than any other sign. More impersonal. Lack of personal identity. Chameleon. Gives indiscriminately. Has difficulty drawing limits. Attuned to the non-tangible.

+   Spiritual. Idealistic. Vulnerable. Empathic. Loving. Giving. Responsive. Sympathetic. Caring. Open. Devoted.

-   Vague. Unfocused. Deceitful. Escapist. Commonly a victim, martyr, or savior. Disorganized. Fanaticism.

Jupiter Rules Pisces

Jupiter in Pisces is imaginative, kind, caring and idealistic. Good listeners. Jupiter attracts good luck when he is giving and compassionate. Helping others brings fulfillment.

Focused, noncritical attitudes and escapism hinder acting on the need for self-improvement.

Mercury is in its Detriment

Mercury in Pisces is sensitive, idealistic, imaginative and evasive. In Pisces, the powers of reason can be confused by daydreaming and self-deception.

Venus is Exalted in Pisces

In Pisces, Venus is gentle, compassionate, romantic and sensitive. Musical and artistic talent. Oversensitivity can lead to hurts that are suffered in silence. A need for love and tenderness. Self-sacrificing may attract you to underdogs.

CHAPTER 20

Key 19 – The Sun

The stage of spiritual unfoldment represented by Key 19 is *Regeneration*.

Key 19 is The Sun. The activity of the Sun is a direct manifestation of the Originating Principle of the universe. The radiant energy of our day star is a particular expression of the universal radiance. It provides substance for the formation of all terrestrial bodies. It is also the power source for all movements of matter on the surface of this globe.

The invisible Spiritual Sun is shown in the upper right-hand corner of Key 0, the Fool. The power of our Sun is identical to that of the spiritual Sun. Still, our day star is only the physical presence of something greater, which shines through all suns and stars and is eternal, whether manifested in physical form or not.

The Sun is pictured with eight salient or pointed and eight wavy rays. Each ray is divided by a line, so the total number suggested is 2 X 16, or 32. This is the number of Paths of Wisdom or aspects of conscious energy.

Our Sun collects and distributes power which gives us light and life. It symbolizes the conscious energy, the source and mover of all terrestrial activities. It is not a blind, purely mechanical or chemical force. It is a living energy akin to ourselves. Physically and mentally, we are sprung from it and belong to the same genus, though we are members of another species. Ageless Wisdom says the Sun is a focus of living consciousness, a being rather than a thing. One might as well try to sum up George Washington by cataloging his physical characteristics to say that the sun is nothing more than the fusion of Hydrogen to release energy and light.

From the sun fall 13 Hebrew Yods (י). In the colored Tarot, they are orange, the hue associated with solar force in our color scale. The same color is used in India to represent *Prana*, the fundamental energy of the universe.

Their number, 13, refers particularly to two Hebrew words having this number, Unity (אחד) and Love (אהבה). This indicates the occult doctrine that the force which unites and combines all things in this world is derived from the Sun and is the attractive power that finds emotional expression in love.

Yod is numerical 10. The 13 letters stand for the number 130. This is the value of several Hebrew words whose English meanings are:

1. Ayin (עין), the Eye, name of the letter on Key 15, The Devil;
2. (הצלה) Deliverance. See Esther 4:14;
3. (מלאך הגאל) Angel of Redemption;
4. The Pillars (עמודי), i.e., Jachin and Boaz;
5. (סלם) A ladder or staircase. Jacob's ladder.

To the inventors of the Tarot, the 13 Yods represented the power that seems like an adversary because we misunderstand it. In truth, this power sets us free, renews our lives, and delivers us from evil. Thus it is truly the Angel of Redemption. The pillars, Jachin and Boaz, represent its dual activities, which Solomon set up before the temple door. These are pictured in Tarot as the pillars of the High Priestess. This power works on various planes, represented in occult fraternities by degrees through which the initiate advances. In the Bible, Jacob's ladder and the diagram of the Tree of Life in the Qabalah represent this system of progressive unfoldment.

In Key 19, the sunflowers represent the manifestation of the solar force in the organic world below man. Four flowers are open, and the fifth is about to bloom. They represent four steps in the upward evolution of the physical embodiment of the Sun's power. These are the mineral kingdom, the vegetable kingdom, animal life, and human life at the level of the average human being. The sunflower about to open symbolizes the completion of the Great Work in regenerated humanity – the Adepts and Masters.

The wall represents the erroneous conception of physical substance, built up by human imagination from sense experience. What we sense is real. Hence the wall is built of stones, not of brick. Yet we mistake the meaning of our sensations. The five courses of the wall correspond to the five main physical senses. They are a barrier to further progress if we rely wholly upon them.

The children, a boy and a girl, just at the beginning of adolescence, represent the unfolding of regenerated human consciousness in the two aspects constituting human personality – self-consciousness (boy) and subconsciousness (girl). In regeneration, the human aspect of subconsciousness is renewed, and the Great Work does more than merely bring animal nature under control. The reconciliation of the Man and the Woman in us is pictured here. When we become "a little child," the man-child of self-consciousness and the woman-child of subconsciousness are regenerated.

The children dance in a fairy ring of two concentric circles, forming a solar symbol (☉). It represents the limitations of physical existence. The message is:

So long as we remain on the physical plane, we do not transcend those limitations.

We do not need to. Health, happiness, and success are not to be sought elsewhere. We may experience them here. So likewise, wisdom, Truth, and Beauty do not abide in some other sphere. Unless we learn to discover them on the physical plane, we shall not find them at all.

The power we employ is not limited to physical existence. This symbolism contradicts the old, lying doctrines that lead men to neglect their world while engaging in vain endeavors to enter an imagined heaven. The Great Secret (which remains a secret, even though we declare it openly) is that physical existence is a spiritual fact.

Practical Instruction

Spiritual consciousness is the Stone of the Wise and the goal of the Great Work. Spiritual consciousness is an awakening to the meaning of what material consciousness supposes to be "nothing but" physical existence. It is a recognition of the spiritual substance of this world. Remember from Key 8, Strength, The Secret to All Spiritual Activities, that all activities on the physical plane are spiritual.

Use Key 19 to awaken your consciousness that you are a Child of the Sun. When this knowledge comes, it wells up in our hearts as a song of joy, and we turn from the limitations of the senses to the freedom of spiritual knowing.

Letter Resh - ר

The letter name Resh (ריש) means face and head. In ancient Egypt, Horus the Elder is visualized as the face of the sun.

The Number 19

In numbers, the end of a cycle is represented by 9 and the beginning by 1. Hence, Key 19 is the Hermit (Key 9) manifesting through the Magician (Key 1).

The Hermit stands for a goal. We work toward it. All practical occultism aims at reaching the height whereon the Hermit stands. The tools we use to reach the goal are derived from the One Source. We apply them through mental activities symbolized by the Magician. The result of this application brings about the result pictured by Key 19. Note that the Magician and the Hermit (Virgo, ruled by Mercury) are related to Mercury.

The Sun

☉

The sense of individuality. Hero archetype. Creative energy, radiant inner self (attunement of soul). Essential values. The urge to be and create. Need to be recognized and to express self. The source of will, vitality, and personal power. The qualities of leadership and authority. The center and power of self. The person's purpose and direction in life.

The Sun is your life force energy that lights up the rest of your astrological chart. By house and sign, the Sun shows what you are under your persona (Ascendant).

+   Radiation of spirit. Creative and loving pouring forth of self.

-   Pride. Excessive desire to be special can lead to self-importance and arrogance.

The Sun's Dignities

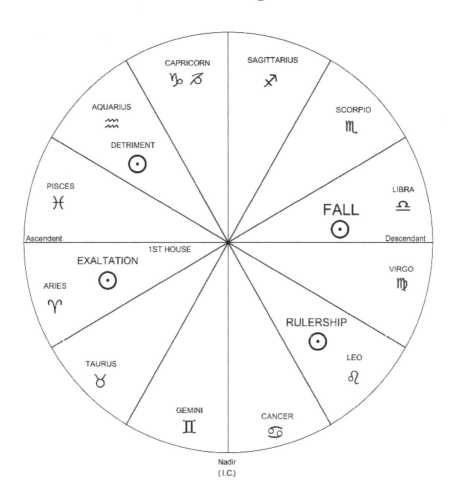

Sun Rules Leo

Expresses self with warmly radiant vitality and needs to be noticed. Creative energy is colored by a sense of drama. Natural leader. Radiates confidence and encouragement to others; can vitalize any enterprise. Pride is a dominant personality characteristic. It cannot be pushed around, but flattery can help motivate. However, enthusiasm needs to be tempered with patience.

Sun is in its Detriment in Aquarius

Creative energy is directed toward the society in welfare and theoretical concepts. Original and Independent. Self-disciplined and responsible. Eccentric and unconventional. Radiates friendly, people-oriented mental energy. Expression of individuality can be deterred by self-effacement, over-concentration on duty, or aimless rebellion. An overly strong Saturn influence can lead to brooding, depression, and self-pity.

Sun is Exalted Aries

Radiates forceful, confident vitality. Enterprising and ambitious. Competitive. The forceful assertion of individuality is necessary for self-expression. Energetic leadership. Explorer, pioneer, the first to begin an adventure; quickly grasp essentials. Maybe insensitive to other people's needs but rarely holds a grudge.

Sun in its Fall in Libra

Creative energy is directed toward interpersonal relationships and initiating ideas. Diplomacy. Needs to be recognized for impartiality, fairness, kindness, and ability to harmonize opposing energies. Constant urge to create balance in one's relationships and lifestyle. The sense of individuality can be obliterated through over-concentration on pleasing others.

CHAPTER 21

Key 20 – Judgment – Pluto

The stage of spiritual unfoldment represented by Key 20 is *Realization*. At this stage, the human consciousness is on the verge of blending with the Universal Consciousness, hence the idea of a resurrection of the new birth. The limiting factors of this world of name and form represented by the coffins are put away. This is accomplished by vibratory activity controlled by the Life Breath, as conveyed by the symbolism of the angel blowing the trumpet.

Perpetual Intelligence is assigned to Key 20. This is an awareness that human life is not temporal but eternal. Participation in this consciousness was the object of the ancient Mysteries. The founders of those Mysteries understood that this type of knowledge results from specific training, whereby the natural man is transformed into a higher species of being.

In the mysteries, there is always a reference to Fire in connection with the experience of Eternal Consciousness. An imperfect experience of this kind led Dr. Bucke to write his book Cosmic Consciousness. Describing his own brief glimpse of this higher knowledge, he speaks of rosy light, so he definitely perceived that he thought there must be a fire in the vicinity.

Ezekiel's and St. John's visions identified the Divine Presence with Fire. The Chaldean Oracles describe various stages of the Great Work, completed by a vision of a cloud of Fire, whirling and folding itself upon itself.

When this is perceived, say the Oracles, "Hear thou the Voice of the Fire."

The real Actor in this divine event is not the man. Instead, it is the One-Spirit, like a devouring fire, consuming the sense of separate identity and releasing us from the bonds of time and space.

The title, Judgment, implies completion, decision, and termination. The Life-power never forgets anything it has begun. Its perfect self-recollection is the basis of all personal activity written on the scroll of the High Priestess, the Book of the Law. Not one jot of Law shall pass away until all be fulfilled. The work of that Law through human action is symbolized by Key 11. This perfect law of compensation brings all manifestations to their fulfillment. Since all manifestations begin in the Will-to-Good, all are eventually destined to manifest the goodness since the Goal and the Source are not two, but ONE.

This is the final state of personal consciousness. The last Key of the Tarot, The World, represents what is beyond any personal condition. But in the situation pictured in Key 20, the condition of "I and another" is still to be seen, which disappears in the perfect unity symbolized by Key 21.

The angel above the figures conceals a geometrical statement of the Fourth Dimension. The whole figure is drawn so that the surrounding cloud defines a circle, containing two smaller circles to make figure 8. Hence this geometrical design represents Eternity (the circle) and dominion (figure 8). This figure is employed in Ouspensky's *Tertium Organum* to represent the Fourth Dimension.

The angel is Gabriel, attributed to the Sephirah Yesod (Foundation), or the Sphere of the Moon. Gabriel is the presiding genius of that element of Water. He is also the active principle behind the apparently passive figure of the High Priestess.

His trumpet represents the specialization of the Life-Breath in sound or vibration. Seven great sounds, each corresponding to one of the planets or interior stars (chakras), are represented by seven rays descending from the trumpet. Twelve rays of light represent the zodiac signs.

The square banner is another reference to the Fourth Dimension. The cross upon it is one form of the Tav (ת) letter on Key 21. The cross upon the square banner symbolizes measurement and reasoned conclusions because correct judgment depends upon the right reasoning and the ability to weigh and measure. Yet the cross is red, the color of Mars, to indicate that self-consciousness must perform an *action* to reach the state of consciousness symbolized by Key 20.

The mountains in the background are snow-covered, like the heights whereon the Fool and the Hermit stand. They represent abstract thought, which finds its purest expression in mathematics.

The sea is the final reservoir of the many Waters, beginning with the robe of the High Priestess in Key 2. This is also the Great Sea of the Qabalists, which they call *Mother*, and is connected with Sephiroth *Binah*, Understanding. Finally, key 20 is a picture of the Life-power's perfect understanding of itself when it manifests in and through a human personality.

Three coffins float on the sea. They are made of stone to represent the physical plane. They are rectangular to show three dimensions.

The three human figures stand upright in the coffins. The line of their bodies is thus at right angles to the bottoms of the coffins. This detail indicates the mathematical definition of the Fourth Dimension – the dimension at right angles to the other three.

The flesh of the rising figures is gray to show that they are not on the physical plane of existence. Gray is the result of the blending of complementary colors. Hence, the symbolism represents overcoming the pair of opposites on the physical plane. Gray also symbolizes the astral plane and represents wisdom.

The woman is the active figure of the three. She receives the influence of the magical vibrations coming from the trumpet. Her uplifted hands represent the sublimation of subconscious activities.

The man stands with hands folded on his breast. He looks up in silent adoration but does nothing because the activity has been transferred from self-consciousness to subconsciousness.

The child stands, giving the traditional Typhon or Apophis the Destroyer sign. He represents the rebirth of mastering the destructive principle, personified in Ancient Egyptian as Apophis.

Thus the three figures represent an ancient mystery formula, which ends with the names of Isis, Apophis, and Osiris. The initials of the three names are I A O or Yaho, one of the most powerful words of power. It directly connects with the controlled employment of sound vibration in ways that make immediate use of the Fourth Dimension, even though most initiates trained in using this mystical word are unaware of it.

Practical Instruction

Key 20 sets the pattern for your own personal realization of immortality. It calls forth the subconscious activities which result in this final liberation. It will aid you in realizing that, even now, you are living in the Fourth Dimension. Eternity, of which time, as measured by man, is merely a partial expression. Key 20 will aid you in understanding that you live in eternity and share the omnipresence which is part of your true make-up. Because Eternity is the foundation of your personal life as a free Spirit, you are neither bound by time nor place.

The Number 20

The number 20 shows the Fiery Intelligence (Key 0) working through the Uniting Intelligence (Key 2).

In gematria, *d'o* (דיו) is numerically 20. It means *fluid darkness, ink*. Darkness is an ancient symbol of subconscious forces and activities.

Because eleven (11) and twenty (20) reduce to 2 (1 + 1 = 2). In Tarot, the High Priestess (2), Justice (11), and Judgment (20) are three aspects of a single manifestation of the Life-power.

The Letter Shin - ש

Shin means tooth or fang. The suggestion is a serpent's tooth, whereby deadly poison is injected into the veins of the snake's victim. The power by means of which liberation is attained, and the supernal consciousness realized, is compared to a venomous serpent.

He who enters into the Perpetual Intelligence or Conscious Immortality symbolized by Key 20 finds out that he has not so much attained that consciousness as his lesser consciousness has been assimilated by the higher order of knowing.

This assimilation requires the old self to *die before the New Self may be born*. Nobody can exercise the higher occult powers and remain an ordinary human being. The First Matter on which we perform the alchemical operation of sublimation is our own consciousness. We must lose our lives to find them.

The Three Mother Letters

Shin (ש pronounced sheen) is the third of the three Mother letters of the Hebrew alphabet.

Hebrew		Tarot	Element
Aleph	א	Key 0	Root of Air
Mem	מ	Key 12	Root of Water
Shin	ש	Key 20	Root of Fire

Cabalists call Sheen the Holy Letter. Sheen is numerically 300, and this is the value of *Ruach Elohim* (רוח אלהים), the Divine Life-Breath.

Fire and Spirit are also associated with Aleph (א). Aleph also symbolizes Ruach, the Life-Breath and the Fiery Intelligence. Thus there is an underlying correspondence between Key 0 and Key 20.

Astrology

In astrology, the planets are divided into categories.

The Lights – The Sun and Moon

The Sun and Moon are the luminaries. They are not technically planets, but in astrology, they are the two most "personal planets."

The Personal Planets

These are planets that move fairly quickly through the chart. They include the two lights (Sun and Moon), Mercury, Venus, and Mars. These are the bodies whose orbits are closest to that of the Earth and, therefore, closest to our physical being. Personal planets are the ones that embody our core personality, fundamental archetypes, and basic drives as humans.

The Social Planets – Jupiter and Saturn

The social planets bridge the gap between the personal and the outer planets. They are the furthest away planets that the naked eye can see from Earth. They represent themes that each of us encounters in life, but ones that go above and beyond us as individuals. Their interpretations are more impersonal and based on our larger cultural environment.

Transpersonal Planets

Uranus – Neptune – Pluto

The generational or transpersonal planets are beyond Saturn. The transpersonal planets are slower moving and represent generational trends. They are also associated with transcending the material world and connecting to broader universal energies.

Transpersonal planets are considered "higher octave planets."

Planet	Higher Octave
Uranus	Mercury
Neptune	Venus
Pluto	Mars

Generally speaking, transpersonal planets don't directly act on an individual but on a whole generation and set societal trends. However, if a transpersonal planet is tightly aspecting or conjunct a personal planet (Pluto conjunct the Sun), you will be very intimate with Pluto's energy.

Pluto - ♇

Principal of elimination & purification of all toxins. Periodic cleansing. Healing. Taboos & secrets. Telling the truth. Transformation. Death & rebirth. Deep shock & spiritual crisis. Area of greatest change. Soul Intent. Obsession & compulsive acts. Spiritual awakening & healing. Powers of rejuvenation. Utilization of power. Sexual/spiritual fusion. Transformation through elimination & destruction. Surrender. Letting go. Domination. Fear of being devoured. Seduction.

+ Ability to surrender to a higher power. Ability to dissolve attachments.

- Obsessiveness. Manipulation. Vampirism. Controlling. The projection of the inner need for change onto others. Misuse of power. When neglected, the "loss of soul" & personal power.

Pluto Co-Rules Scorpio

In modern times, Pluto was in Scorpio between 1983 and 1995. This is Generation Y or the Millennials.

The Pluto in Scorpio generation has loss, abandonment, and betrayal issues. This loss is typically reflected by the loss of one or both parents – whether physically or emotionally.

Pluto manifests as a trauma that leaves the individual lacking direction and safety. The challenge of the Millennials is to find their own inner guidance.

CHAPTER 22

Key 21 – The World – Saturn

Key 21 represents the last stage of spiritual unfoldment, *Cosmic Consciousness*.

This Key represents the uses of limitation. It shows that the dance of life is carried on using the form-building power that gives us difficulties. It is that power which enables us to measure and to know with exactness and precision. Its influence is limiting and restrictive, but this is never malefic unless we allow it to use us instead of our using it. Remember that concentration is an act of limitation. Yet, this power is the basis upon which all science is founded.

The letter on Key 21 is Tav (ת), meaning signature or mark. In ancient Hebrew, it was often written like the plus sign (+) in arithmetic.

As a signature, Tav implies security, pledge, and guarantee. The signature makes a business contract valid. The sign of Tav is the final seal and witness of the Great Work.

The direction attributed to Tav is the Center, called The Palace of Holiness in the midst. The Hebrew word for "palace" is (היכל), *Haikal* and its number is 65, the value of Adonai (אדני), Lord. Therefore, Adonai is the ruling principle that dwells at the CENTER.

Administrative Intelligence is assigned to Tav because the Lord's consciousness – the mental state of the Originating and Directive Principle of the universe – administers every detail of cosmic activity.

When a human completes the Great Work, contemporaries think the individual has gained unusual control over their environment. They know better.

They have identified themselves with the central, directive PRINCIPLE of the universe. Because this has occurred, every thought, word, and deed is an immediate, undistorted expression of the Conscious Energy which administers the laws of nature. He has not gained power. They give free expression to the One Power, the central reality of every human life.

When we participate in the cosmic government, we enter the kingdom of heaven as fully enfranchised citizen who takes an active part in the execution of the laws. Nature obeys us because we express THAT, both Author and Lord of nature.

The planet Saturn is assigned to Tav. Your personal "Saturn" is the interior star or chakra center at the base of the spine where the serpent-power is coiled.

In mythology, Saturn is the father of the gods and eats his children. The meaning is that the mode of consciousness typified by Saturn and Tav swallows up all other modes of consciousness.

To give any adequate verbal expression to this is impossible. Nevertheless, we do what we can when we say there is no trace of otherness in the all-embracing Divine Consciousness.

Every human being who has tried to express his own experience of this consciousness has reported that everything disappears but the sense of IDENTITY or ONENESS. Such statements are unintelligible to ordinary men and women. Yet, the fact that all seers agree to use this language indicates they have had a common experience. Difficult as it is to imagine such an experience, reasoning suggests that all-inclusive consciousness is free from the ideas of "I am I, and the universe is another."

This is not easy to explain. Perhaps you may grasp the idea if we say the final outcome of the Great Work is really a recollection of powers most persons have forgotten they possess.

Among these powers is an extension of consciousness beyond the body's limits into the forms constituting one's environment. In this consciousness, the whole universe is perceived as being the ONE BODY of the ONESELF. To realize this is to be aware that the directive CENTER of the whole cosmic activity field dwells in human hearts.

The title, "The World," is a translation of the Hebrew *olahm* (עולם), meaning *eternity, universe*, and *world*. The oldest significance of this word is *that which is hidden or veiled*.

The title of Key 21 also indicates what may be termed "world consciousness." He who learns to express Administrative Intelligence is in tune with the universe.

The four animals are the same as those of Key 10. They are associated with the fixed signs of the zodiac. They represent the fixed conditions in which all manifestation takes place. They are also symbols of the four letters of IHVH (יהוה), of the four elements, and of four great planes of existence. The idea suggested by their positions in the corners of the Key is that every event is included within the ALL.

The wreath is an ellipse, eight units high and five units wide. This presents a formula for the approximate squaring of the circle, and the sum of the numbers 5 and 8 gives 13, which denotes Unity and Love. It refers to the Life-Power as the fundamental principle of form. Since a wreath is a man's work, it refers to man's use of this power for creating.

The wreath comprises twenty-two groups of three leaves, eleven groups on either side. The leaves represent the forces of organic life arranged by art to conform to the geometrical basis of creation.

This wreath is really a zero-sign. It indicates that the World and the No-Thing are not two things, but ONE. The World is the way the No-Thing presents itself to our minds.

The wreath is fastened at the top and bottom by two horizontal figures 8. The same symbol is shown in Keys 1 and 8. Here the symbol is red to show that the power of the Infinite is brought into action above and below, that is, in consciousness and in subconsciousness.

The dancing figure is the Woman who has appeared throughout this series. It is so drawn that her head and hands are at the angles of a triangle, apex upward, while her legs form a cross. Thus the figure suggests the alchemical symbol for Sulfur, a triangle over a cross.

The woman is the embodiment of the fiery Life-power. Her dance suggests the Law of Rhythm, which is everywhere at work. She dances on air, just as the Yods (') hang in the air in Keys 16, 18 and 19. This is a reference to the occult doctrine that the foundation is SPIRIT.

The spirals in her hands represent integration and disintegration since they are turning in opposite directions. They symbolize the dual operations of the One Force. They emit flashes of light. They are symbols of the universal spiral force which enters into all activities.

The central figure appears feminine, but the legs have a masculine appearance, revealing that the figure is really androgynous. THAT WHICH IS appears now as Father and again as Mother. Yet THAT is limited by neither gender. It includes and transcends both male and female.

The violet veil is shaped like the Hebrew letter Kaph (כ) assigned to Key 10. The meaning here is that the mechanism of the universe, which seems like a system of wheels within wheels, hides the truth that whatever exists is an expression of Love and Life. We are not merely witnesses, observing the operations of a machine. We are living centers through which an organism's ruling and administrative consciousness is known.

They who find the CENTER also find the TEMPLE or PALACE OF THE KING. They who find the SELF find the WORLD-RULER. They who know what is behind the veil of mechanism know that the ONE POWER is the LIFE-POWER and the LOVE-POWER.

This is the final revelation, the consciousness reached at the end of the seven stages of enfoldment. This end is also a new beginning.

Once the CENTER is found and personal consciousness is swallowed up in realizing IDENTITY or UNION, the end, or true purpose, of existence is experienced. They who enter this happy state's perfect bliss and wisdom become one who knows but cannot tell.

For most persons, this is a brief ecstasy. Yet one never forgets it. By it, one's whole outlook is changed. More than this, the experience never comes until one has undergone, through the agency of subconsciousness, many alterations in the personal vehicle.

The individual becomes a new creature, a member of a different species. However, the individual cannot transmit the newly acquired characteristics to posterity utilizing the reproductive process. Yet, by a subtle redirection of our sexual energy, we beget spiritual children.

By this, we mean that **an Adept or a Master can**, for a short time, increase the receptivity of specially selected persons. The adept can take one "close to the kingdom of God" and communion with something of their own vision.

This is the secret of the great leaders who have brought enlightenment to humanity. They awaken us from our dream of sense. They stir us deeply. They cannot tell us what they know, but they can give us eyes wherewith to see.

Practical Instruction

Key 21 appears to be the end of the series. However, Key 0 follows Key 21. Thus the Tarot is a never ceasing cycle. There are always other steps to take and a higher goal to strive for. As you continue in your search for truth, you will find the principles embodied in the tarot will be those upon which you must rely for your guidance in every plane of existence because evolution and spiritual growth manifest Cosmic Law.

The Number 21

The number 21 is the sum of the digits from 0 to 6 inclusive. Therefore Key 21 is a sum of all the ideas in the series from the Fool (Key 0) to the Lovers (Key 6).

Also, 21 expresses the power of 1 (self-consciousness) through the agency of 2 (subconsciousness).

Yet, in Key 21, self-consciousness is not personal. Instead, it is the self-awareness of the ONE IDENTITY, and the subconsciousness through which it works is the all-inclusive subconscious level of the Life Power's being.

Saturn Attributes

The principles of contraction, limitation, restriction, and discipline. Sorrow and hardships. Father and authority issues. Work, Effort, and Karma. The principle of form and definition. Personal identity, security, and inertia. Saturn motivates through fear. No pain, no gain. How one seeks to establish and preserve self. Where effort, hard work and responsibility are required to succeed. Infantile wound. Shortcomings and defects. Fears, commitments and responsibilities. Being your own parent. The power to manifest. Long-term endurance.

+   Disciplined effort. Acceptance of duties and responsibilities. Patience. Organization. Reliability.

-   Self-restriction through too much reliance on self and lack of faith. Rigidity. Coldness. Defensiveness and negativity.

Saturn's Dignities

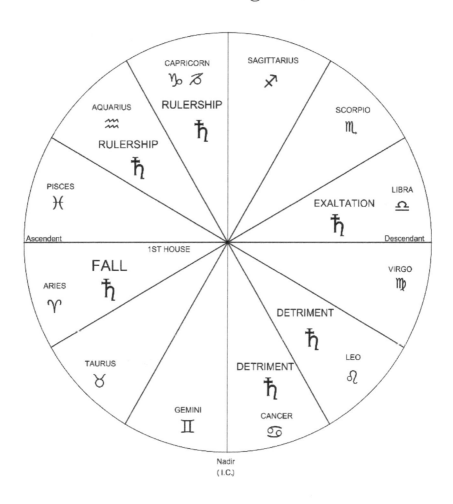

Saturn Rules Capricorn

Persistent, calculating, careful and practical. Good organizers and high achievers. Seeks to establish and preserve self by attaining one's ambitions, authority, and societal position. Strongly disciplined efforts expended toward planning the fulfillment of one's responsibilities. Overly-developed organizing ability can lead to attempts to control all situations too tightly. Urge to defend integrity through determination, hard work, and cautious behavior. Excessive fear of disapproval can hinder the full achievement of one's aims. Deep-seated need to be a reliable person and depend on one's own resources.

Saturn is in its Detriment in Cancer

Saturn is a somber and reserved planet. Cancer is an emotional sign. Saturn in Cancer is reserved in its display of love and emotions. Isolation and shyness. Melancholy. Saturn in Cancer is challenged to respect emotions without blocking them until they spill out uncontrolled.

Saturn is in its Detriment in Leo

Saturn in Leo can experience limitations on this ego self, fear of self-expression and lack of confidence.

Saturn in Leo worries that it's not good enough and behaving irresponsibly. As a result, Saturn's need for responsible behavior sometimes censors its expression.

Saturn is Exalted in Libra

Saturn in Libra is disciplined, responsible and serious but also has a sense of justice and fairness. Saturn in Libra makes good lawyers, judges, mathematicians, and engineers since they understand relationships on human and scientific levels. Moreover, Saturn in Libra artist gives form and beauty through proper balance and proportion.

Fear (Saturn) of committed partnership (Libra) can hinder achievement and prevent a sense of satisfying intimacy. Therefore, disciplined effort is put into maintaining relationships. Commitments, promises, and duties are honored and can bring deep satisfaction.

Saturn is in its Fall in Aries

Aries is Cardinal Fire that likes to lead. Aries's motto is, "Let's do something, even if it's wrong." They learn from their mistakes and move on. However, Saturn Aries needs to think before it acts. The need for exercise to release pent-up impatience and irritation.

APPENDIX 1 - TABLES

The Hebrew Letters and Values

	Title	Hebrew			Meaning	#
0	The Fool	Aleph	א		Ox	1
1	The Magician	Beth	ב	F	house	2
2	The Moon	Gimel	ג	i	foot	3
3	The High Priestess	Daleth	ד	n a l	door	4
4	The Emperor	Heh	ה		arms raised	5
5	The Hierophant	Vav	ו		nail or peg	6
6	The Lovers	Zain	ז		sword, sickle	7
7	The Chariot	Cheth	ח		fence	8
8	Strength	Teth	ט		Serpent, coil	9
9	The Hermit	Yod	י		hand	10
10	Wheel of Fortune	Kaph	כ	ך	open palm of hand	20
11	Justice	Lamed	ל		shepherd's staff	30
12	Hanged Man	Mem	מ	ם	water	40
13	Death	Nun	נ	ן	seed sprout	50
14	Temperance	Samekh	ס		thorn	60
15	The Devil	Ayin	ע		an eye	70
16	The Tower	Peh	פ	ף	a mouth	80
17	The Star	Tzaddi	צ	ץ	net, snare	90
18	The Moon	Qoph	ק		coil, circuit	100
19	The Sun	Resh	ר		a head	200
20	Judgment	Shin	ש		teeth, fangs	300
21	The World	Tau	ת		Mark	400

The final letters are used when they come at the end of the word. For example, Aleph (א) spelled in full is (אלף).

Aleph (א), Lamed (ל), and final Peh (ף). Notice that Peh is in its final form at the end of the word.

Key	Title	Color	Musical Note
0	The Fool	Yellow	E Natural
1	The Magician	Yellow	E Natural
2	The Moon	Blue	G Sharp
3	The High Priestess	Green	F Sharp
4	The Emperor	Red	C Natural
5	The Hierophant	Red-Orange	C Sharp
6	The Lovers	Orange	D Natural
7	The Chariot	Orange-Yellow	D Sharp
8	Strength	Yellow	E Natural
9	The Hermit	Yellow-Green	F Natural
10	The Wheel of Fortune	Violet	A Sharp
11	Justice	Green	F Sharp
12	The Hanged Man	Blue	G Sharp
13	Death	Blue-Green	G Natural
14	Temperance	Blue	G Sharp
15	The Devil	Blue-Violet	A Natural
16	The Tower	Red	C Natural
17	The Star	Violet	A Sharp
18	The Moon	Violet-Red	B Natural
19	The Sun	Orange	D Natural
20	Judgment	Red	C Natural
21	The World	Blue-Violet	A Natural

PAUL FOSTER CASE BOOKS

1. SEVEN STEPS IN PRACTICAL OCCULTISM

2. AN INTRODUCTION TO THE TAROT AND ASTROLOGY

3. TAROT FUNDAMENTALS

4. TAROT INTERPRETATIONS

5. THE MASTER PATTERN

6. THE THIRTY-TWO PATHS OF WISDOM

7. THE TREE OF LIFE

8. THE NEOPIIYTE RITUALS OF PAUL FOSTER CASE

9. THE ATTUNEMENT RITUALS OF PAUL FOSTER OF CASE

10. THE SECOND ORDER RITUALS OF PAUL FOSTER CASE

WADE COLEMAN BOOKS

1. SEPHER SAPPHIRES Volume 1

2. SEPHER SAPPHIRES Volume 2

3. THE ASTROLOGY WORKBOOK

4. MAGIC OF THE PLANETS

5. THE MAGICAL PATH

6. THE ZODIAC OF DENDARA EGYPT

7. ATHANASIUS KIRCHER'S QUADRIVIUM

To contact the author,

DENDARA_ZODIAC@protonmail.com

Made in United States
Troutdale, OR
11/17/2023